"Religious liberty is a first and fundamental freedom that the Constitution intends as protection for all citizens of the United States, whether they are religious or not. Today that freedom is increasingly endangered as intolerance toward Christianity and other religions threatens the mission of faith-based institutions that pursue the common good. In *Free to Serve*, Stephen Monsma and Stanley Carlson-Thies offer proactive remedies that nourish the hope of principled pluralism and promote a civil society in which people of all faiths, or none, enjoy expansive freedom."

—**Philip G. Ryken**, president, Wheaton College

"Stephen V. Monsma is the dean of social science scholars who study faith-based organizations and Stanley Carlson-Thies is the nation's most passionate yet nuanced public voice for institutional religious freedom. Together they have produced this timely, readable, and intellectually serious book. Whether one embraces or eschews their preferred policy prescriptions, the authors make their case in civic-minded ways that leaven and enlighten our increasingly shrill and polarized church-state discourse."

—**John J. DiIulio Jr.**, University of Pennsylvania; first director, White House Office of Faith-Based and Community Initiatives

"Sobering and significant, *Free to Serve* outlines the very real threats to religious freedom for all faith-based organizations. If you believe your faith should extend beyond the walls of your place of worship, you simply must read this outstanding book."

—**Peter Greer**, president and CEO, HOPE International; coauthor of *Mission Drift*

"The threat to religious liberty grows more intense, even as the debate over the meaning of religious freedom escalates. Monsma and Carlson-Thies speak into this critical moment, unveiling errors in the four common faith-based assumptions of our day. *Free to Serve* examines the unintended consequences of violating religious freedom and offers hope for a society where individual beliefs are fully expressed and diversity in those beliefs is respected and protected."

—**Tami Heim**, president and CEO, Christian Leadership Allian

"*Free to Serve* is an important and timely book. The authors' call t principled pluralism—allowing divergent religious groups latitude t live out the implications of their faith in the public square—is a vita message. Cultural pressure to privatize faith to the narrow sphere o the sacraments is bad news not only for people of faith but also for ou nation as a whole."

—**Alec Hill**, president, InterVarsity Christian Fellowship/USA

"In our pluralistic society, the only way we can get along with one another is by respecting the rights of groups with whom we don't necessarily agree. This book explains how religious institutions caring for our communities risk losing their character as faith-based organizations. We have to protect the rights of everyone in our society if we are to protect the rights of anyone. This is an important book for our times."

—**Richard Stearns**, president, World Vision US;
author of *The Hole in Our Gospel* and *Unfinished*

"An excellent, readable book on a crucial topic. The next decade may very well see more ferocious—and hugely important—battles over religious freedom than at any time in recent decades. This book is one of the very best guides to the threat and the solution. A must-read for anyone interested in preserving our country's historic stance on religious freedom."

—**Ronald J. Sider**, Palmer Seminary, Eastern University

"Monsma and Carlson-Thies present a timely and compelling case for how the United States can navigate the current changes to social norms by proposing that society value and give equal credence to the ideas of all religions and the nonreligious alike. Higher education presents one such successful model. Christian colleges and universities have long been part of a vibrant and diverse community of higher education in the United States. Such a pluralistic model, which has produced the best higher education system in the world, serves as a guide for how a society that is open to free thought, belief, and practice cannot only survive, but thrive."

—**Shirley V. Hoogstra, JD**, president, Council for Christian
Colleges and Universities

"Today's complacency is tomorrow's captivity. As one of our God-given rights, religious liberty stands under unprecedented assault. *Free to Serve* provides a clarion call and prophetic prescription for those committed to never sacrificing truth on the altar of expediency."

—**Samuel Rodriguez**, president, NHCLC/CONELA,
Hispanic Evangelical Association

"Anyone who cares about the state of religious freedom in America should read this book. First Amendment protections for faith-based organizations are undergoing seismic change, pushing us in a dangerous direction. The authors have accurately surveyed the shifting landscape and where our first freedoms may be headed. *Free to Serve* is a cautionary yet hopeful assessment of the future of religious liberty."

—**David Nammo**, executive director and CEO, Christian Legal Society

FREE
TO
SERVE

PROTECTING THE RELIGIOUS FREEDOM
OF FAITH-BASED ORGANIZATIONS

★

STEPHEN V. MONSMA
AND
STANLEY W. CARLSON-THIES

Brazos Press
a division of Baker Publishing Group
Grand Rapids, Michigan

Published by Brazos Press
a division of Baker Publishing Group
P.O. Box 6287, Grand Rapids, MI 49516-6287
www.brazospress.com

Printed in the United States of America

Library of Congress Cataloging-in-Publication Data
Monsma, Stephen V., 1936–
    Free to serve : protecting the religious freedom of faith-based organizations / Stephen V. Monsma and Stanley Carlson-Thies.
        pages cm
    Includes bibliographical references and index.
    ISBN 978-1-58743-373-3 (pbk.)
    1. United States—Religion. 2. Freedom of religion—United States. 3. Faith-based human services—United States. 4. Religious institutions—Unites States. I. Title.
BL2525.M664 2015
323.44′20973—dc23   2015023298

15 16 17 18 19 20 21   7 6 5 4 3 2 1

Contents

130755

Preface

This book has grown out of our direct involvement with faith-based organizations active in the world of providing needed services to the public. One of us is a researcher who for years has studied faith-based organizations by visiting their programs, interviewing their staff members and clients, and analyzing the effectiveness of their work. Also, one of us is actively involved in the development of public policy in Washington, DC, as it affects faith-based organizations. He played a key role in the addition of the "charitable choice" provision to the 1996 Welfare Reform Act, was an official in President George W. Bush's White House Office of Faith-Based and Community Initiatives, served on the church-state taskforce of President Barack Obama's faith-based advisory council, and now is head of the Institutional Religious Freedom Alliance within the Center for Public Justice, an alliance serving faith-based organizations. Our understanding of faith-based organizations—whether nonprofit or for-profit—has been shaped and molded by our hands-on observations of faith-based organizations and direct involvements with their programs, staffs, and leaders.

Out of these experiences we have become increasingly convinced of two things. One is that faith-based organizations are facing—and will increasingly face—threats to their ability freely to follow their deeply held religious convictions. The very convictions that led persons of faith to create their organizations and that continue to shape the services they offer and to motivate their supporters, staffs, and volunteers are under threat. Let no one underestimate the dangers they are facing.

But we are also convinced of a second thing: there is hope. All is far from being lost. We have written this book out of hope—even optimism—not out of fear or despair. In this book we present seven case studies of faith-based organizations—six nonprofit and one for-profit—to illustrate that there are very real threats facing faith-based organizations' religious freedom rights. But these case studies also illustrate how those rights can be—and sometimes already are—protected. The threats are real, but how we as a society finally resolve these threats is yet to be determined.

We also have hope because we are convinced American society is not facing a zero-sum conflict where one side's victory means the other side's loss. The goals of those who are advocating policies harmful to the religious freedom of faith-based organizations can largely be met while also protecting the religious freedom of faith-based organizations. What is needed is a renewal of mutual respect and a recommitment to a pluralist society where we live together, even while continuing to have deep differences. Respect for the religious beliefs and moral convictions of others has always been a defining characteristic of the American way. Our society is becoming increasingly diverse and complex, but we believe that this defining characteristic should and can take on a new life.

It is our hope and prayer that this book will help lead to a renewal of religious freedom, so that—as the title states—faith-based organizations will be free to serve those whom they have been called to serve, and to be able to do so without having to jettison the very faith and faith-based practices that led them to provide services to those in need.

The religious freedom issues we consider here are truly *religious* freedom issues not Catholic, evangelical, Jewish, or Muslim freedom issues. And the protection of religious freedom is a cause in which persons of good will from a nonreligious background can also join. Therefore, we have included in this book six essays written by persons from Roman Catholic, evangelical, Jewish, Muslim, and nonreligious backgrounds. Three are included as "Interludes" between chapters and three appear in chapter 9. Although we do not necessarily agree with all that these essays say, they demonstrate the breadth of concern for religious freedom and how persons of diverse backgrounds come together in support of it.

In writing a book such as this, we acquired many debts along the way, since many hands and minds have played a role in its writing. We especially wish to thank the following persons who read an early version of our manuscript and whose comments saved us from errors and greatly improved the book: Shapri Lo-Maglio of the Council of Christian Colleges and Universities, Steven McFarland of World Vision USA, Michael Moses of the United States Conference of Catholic Bishops, Austin Nimocks of the Alliance Defending Freedom, and Stephanie Summers of the Center for Public Justice. Any remaining errors or shortcomings are, of course, our responsibility alone, not theirs. We also wish to thank the writers of the essays that are included in this book: Kristina Arriaga de Bucholz of the Becket Fund for Religious Liberty, Kim Colby of the Christian Legal Society's Center for Law and Religious Freedom, Nathan Diament of the Orthodox Union Advocacy Center, Douglas Laycock of the University of Virginia School of Law, Hamza Yusuf Hanson and Mahan Hussain Mirza of Zaytuna College, and Tish Harrison Warren, a priest in the Anglican Church in North America. Their contributions have added much to the book and its message.

We also wish to thank the Paul B. Henry Institute for the Study of Christianity and Politics at Calvin College whose financial support helped at several key points, including making possible the essays included in this book. Finally, we wish to acknowledge and thank the team at Baker Publishing Group and its Brazos imprint for their support and encouragement, as well as their editing and production skills. We especially wish to thank Robert Hosack, executive editor at Baker Publishing Group, and Lisa Ann Cockrel, who guided our manuscript through to publication. We also wish to thank Robert Hand for his copyediting skills and Paula Gibson for her cover design.

Stephen V. Monsma, Grand Rapids, Michigan
Stanley W. Carlson-Thies, Washington, DC

1

A Vision for Our Nation

★

We Americans are rightly grateful for our tradition of religious freedom for all. We take pride in the simple, elegant—even if not fully clear—words of the First Amendment: "Congress shall make no law respecting an establishment of religion or prohibiting the free exercise thereof." The Supreme Court has repeatedly, often in ringing words of affirmation, insisted on religious freedom as essential and unassailable. Justice Potter Stewart once penned words that still inspire: "What our Constitution indispensably protects is the freedom of each of us, be he Jew or Agnostic, Christian or Atheist, Buddhist or Freethinker, to believe or disbelieve, to worship or not worship, to pray or keep silent, according to his own conscience, uncoerced and unrestrained by government."[1]

But today there are voices insisting that religious freedom in the United States is at risk, that we are in danger of losing one of our most precious freedoms. Recently the United States Conference of Catholic Bishops Ad Hoc Committee on Religious Liberty declared, "We need, therefore, to speak frankly with each other

1

when our freedoms are threatened. Now is such a time. . . . For religious liberty is under attack, both at home and abroad."[2] Michael McConnell—a former federal Court of Appeals judge, a Stanford law school professor, and an evangelical Protestant—has written, "Much of this traditional [religious] bigotry has subsided. But it has been replaced with a new brand of intolerance for religions that dissent from modern orthodoxies about sexuality, abortion, family structure, or education."[3] The Institutional Religious Freedom Alliance—of which one of us is the head and the other a longtime supporter—was founded because many were convinced that religious freedom is in crucial ways at risk.

At first glance fears for religious freedom in the United States appear to be absurd. After all, our nation is marked by an extremely wide religious diversity. Compared to religious persecution by ISIS and in North Korea, Iran, China, and elsewhere, we are blessed with full and rich religious freedom. Roman Catholic and Protestant churches dot our landscape; Jewish synagogues are a long-established, accepted part of our religious scene; many cities have more than one mosque; and Sikh temples are far from rare—all this with a minimum of controversy.

Nevertheless, we are writing this book because we are convinced that our religious freedom is, in some important ways, in danger in the United States today. This is especially true of faith-based educational, health care, and social service organizations that believers have created in order to live their faith in the public realm.* We are writing to explain the extent and nature of this

---

* It is important to understand that when we use terms, as we do here, such as "the public realm," "the public life of the nation," and "the public square," we are referring to more than government and the political realm. We use these terms not only to refer to state, local, and national governments and their far-reaching activities, but also to what is often referred to as civil society. This is the world of persons and organizations in their roles as providers of educational, health, and social services to the general public (beyond only their own members). Also included are persons and organizations who report, comment on, and seek to influence government and its activities. Thus the news media, news commentators, and public policy research centers (think tanks) are also included.

danger and to point out the path toward more complete religious freedom for all.

Our Vision

At the outset we need to describe our vision of religious freedom for all. It is one where persons of all religious faiths and of none are not only free to worship or refrain from worship as their beliefs require, but also free to live out their faith as citizens active in the public life of the nation and in the faith-based organizations they have formed. In this vision society acknowledges and respects the wide diversity of religious and nonreligious belief systems, perspectives, and organizations. None is favored; none is disfavored. This is where we take our stand. This is what we defend in this book.

This vision for our nation is based on a commitment to religious freedom, pluralism, and tolerance. We chose those words carefully. Religious freedom means, as we just stated, that persons of all religious faiths and of none are free to believe and to act on those beliefs—in their lives as private individuals, as citizens active in the public realm, and as members of organizations of like-minded believers.

This will result in a pluralist society, one where Catholics, evangelicals, Orthodox Jews, Muslims, Sikhs, nonbelievers, and others are free to live as citizens, health care providers, businesspersons, social-service providers, and public officials as led by their religious or nonreligious beliefs. This means there will be faith-based organizations—and sometimes businesses—that differ widely: some colleges will be thoroughly secular in nature, others will be deeply rooted in a particular religious tradition; some health clinics will offer birth control, sterilizations, and abortions, others will refuse to offer any of these; some organizations will advocate for same-sex marriage, others will advocate for only male-female

"We need leaders, and people to support them, who recognize
that the question for this century is not 'how do I win?' but 'how
can we live together?'"[4] —Michael Wear, former White House
staffer during the Obama administration and writer for *The Atlantic*

marriage; some stores will specialize in kosher foods, others will
not. Pluralism says that diversity such as this is to be expected in
a free society.

Pluralism requires tolerance. We must indeed be free to believe
deeply and debate vigorously, yet we also need to learn anew to
live with, respect, and make room in our public policies for our
fellow citizens with whom we have deep differences—and for the
organizations they have formed to live out or express their faiths.
An imposed uniformity is the opposite of freedom, pluralism,
and tolerance.

We do not seek a victory of one side or the other in what has
been called religious culture wars. Rather, we seek common ground
where the beliefs, practices, and organizations of those of all faiths
and of none are respected and their freedoms protected.

This means that, although both of us writing this book are
Christian believers with roots in the evangelical tradition, our
goal is not to privilege our own tradition and its beliefs. We are
pledged to defend as vigorously the religious freedom rights of
our Roman Catholic, Eastern Orthodox, mainline Protestant,
Muslim, Jewish, Buddhist, Hindu, Sikh, and nonbelieving fellow
citizens as we do our own. We seek a public realm that respects
the diversity of belief and practice present in American society,
not one that favors one group's beliefs and practices over those of
others. We believe, as previously stated, in a public square marked
by religious freedom, pluralism, and tolerance.

A public realm such as this requires the nonreligious to show
the same willingness to tolerate and extend freedom rights to

the beliefs, practices, and organizations of the religious that we are asking the religious to extend to the nonreligious and their beliefs, practices, and organizations. Respect and tolerance must go both ways. A society united by mutual respect and the freedom of all persons to practice their beliefs is what we seek. We do not seek a society united by an enforced uniformity of belief and practice—whether those beliefs and practices are religious or secular in nature.

Our Concerns

But isn't the vision we have just described what all Americans aspire to and what, with only a few regrettable exceptions, we in fact have achieved? We recognize there are few problems today with the freedom of religious congregations to celebrate their faith by way of prayers, religious services, and the rituals of their faith. There are also few problems with persons and families living out their various faiths as individuals in the privacy of their own homes. Problems arise, however, when deeply religious persons—in obedience to their faith—put that faith into practice in the world beyond the privacy of their homes or the four walls of their houses of worship. When persons seek to faithfully follow their religious beliefs in the public realms of health care, education, and services

> "A healthy pluralism, one which genuinely respects differences and values them as such, does not entail privatizing religions in an attempt to reduce them to the quiet obscurity of the individual's conscience or to relegate them to the enclosed precincts of churches, synagogues or mosques. This would represent, in effect, a new form of discrimination and authoritarianism."[5] — Pope Francis

to the needy—and sometimes their businesses—and when they form organizations to do so, their religiously based practices are increasingly called into question. This is when religious freedom problems arise.

Much of what we say in this book is rooted in the fact that when the faithful are constricted in their freedom to live their faith in the public realm—even when they are free to worship in their congregations or the privacy of their homes—their religious freedom is being violated. Freedom of religion is more than the freedom of worship. This conclusion is based on the simple fact that an accurate understanding of religion must conclude that religion encompasses much more than the rituals, celebrations, and prayers of worship services. The failure of many to recognize this fact goes a long way to explain why the religious freedom of many faith-based organizations is at risk today.

Note the following four statements.

> Love for widows and orphans, prisoners, and the sick and needy of every kind, is as essential to her [the Church] as the ministry of the sacraments and preaching of the Gospel. The Church cannot neglect the service of charity any more than she can neglect the Sacraments and the Word. . . . These duties presuppose each other and are inseparable.[6]

> Yet we are the carriers of the gospel—the good news that was meant to *change* the world. Belief is not enough. Worship is not enough. Personal morality is not enough. And Christian community is not enough. God has always demanded *more*. . . . Living out our faith privately was never meant to be an option.[7]

> Our faith journey isn't just about showing up on Sunday for a good sermon and good music and a good meal. It's about what we do Monday through Saturday as well. . . . We see this in the life of Jesus Christ. Jesus didn't limit his ministry to the four walls of the church.[8]

Then he will say to those on his left, "Depart from me, you who are cursed, into the eternal fire prepared for the devil and his angels. For I was hungry and you gave me nothing to eat, I was thirsty and you gave me nothing to drink, I was a stranger and you did not invite me in, I needed clothes and you did not clothe me, I was sick and in prison and you did not look after me." They also will answer, "Lord, when did we see you hungry or thirsty or a stranger or needing clothes or sick or in prison, and did not help you?" He will reply, "Truly I tell you, whatever you did not do for one of the least of these, you did not do for me." (Matt. 25:41–45 NIV)

These statements are from Pope Benedict XVI; Richard Stearns, president of the large evangelical international aid agency World Vision; First Lady Michelle Obama; and Jesus Christ. All insist that care of the hurting and needy of this world is an integral part of the Christian faith. It is not a nice "add-on" to the Christian faith but the very heart of it.

Pope Benedict's language is especially striking. In the Catholic tradition, caring for the needy is as essential and integral to the Christian faith as is the celebration of the sacraments and the preaching of the gospel. Jesus himself saw care of the needy as being so integral to the faith, he preached that those who failed to do so were in danger of everlasting separation from God. Christianity is not merely what happens within the walls of churches, as Michelle Obama expresses it. One stretches one's imagination to come up with ways to more strongly and explicitly link worship and the celebration of religious rituals, on the one hand, and, on the other hand, acts of caring for others in need. Both are essential to the practice of the Christian faith. If government would ban or interfere with the practice of the one it would be as much a violation of religious freedom as if it would ban or interfere with the other.

Believers' faith encompasses their private lives, but in almost all religious traditions it also encompasses their public lives as they actively follow their faith's demands in the public world of educating the young, providing services to the sick, helping those in need, and offering goods and services to the public. The well-known evangelical pastor Rick Warren once wrote that religion is much more than worship; it is also "a way of life."[9]

Once one understands that the actual nature of religion extends beyond prayers and worship, one can also recognize the seriousness of our concerns. If religion is not understood for what it actually is, the freedom of religion we as a society proclaim in words is in danger of being limited in practice. Every limitation on people's freedom to freely exercise their religious beliefs is serious. For many, religion lies near the heart of who they are. Their identity and their deepest beliefs are at issue. It is with good reason that freedom of religion is often referred to as our first freedom.

Our concerns, however, are also based on the huge role that faith-based schools, hospitals and health clinics, and charitable organizations play in American society. One of the foremost scholars of nonprofit organizations, Lester Salamon of Johns Hopkins University, has reported that nonprofit organizations are crucial in the provision of social welfare and many other services such as health care, education, international aid, and the arts.[10] He has also documented a less well-known fact: "Religious institutions are near the epicenter of American philanthropy: they absorb well over half of all private charitable contributions, and account for

> "Religion is a large and important part of the nonprofit sector and has given birth to many other nonprofit institutions: health, education, social services, international assistance, advocacy, mutual assistance, and even some cultural and grant-making organizations. Directly and indirectly, religion has been the major formative influence on American's independent sector."[11] —Michael O'Neill, professor emeritus, University of San Francisco

a disproportionate share of the private voluntary effort. . . . No account of the United States nonprofit sector would therefore be complete without some attention to the religious institutions the sector also contains."[12]

The size of the religious nonprofit sector and the vital role it plays in American society mean that when the religious freedom rights of religiously based organizations are threatened, a truly serious religious freedom issue has arisen. Violations of the religious freedom rights of faith-based organizations constitute an interference with the religious freedom of tens of thousands of faith-based organizations. If we ignore such violations, the consequences for those organizations and the persons they serve would be severe. Faith-based organizations and their staffs and supporters would find their ability to follow their religious beliefs in the public realm constricted and limited. They would be slowly squeezed into a more secular mold and lose much of their religious distinctiveness. They would begin to look more and more alike. Many might decide to go out of business since the reason for their existence would be undercut. For the millions they now serve, diversity and choice would suffer.

Also in the case of for-profit businesses, there are some who seek to follow their religiously based beliefs in their business practices. Their practices reflect and are based on their owners' religious beliefs, whether they are those of Orthodox Judaism, evangelical Protestantism, Catholicism, Islam, or some other faith. These owners see their businesses as direct outgrowths or extensions of their faith. They too have run into problems in being able to freely follow their religious beliefs in their business practices. If they would also be squeezed into a mold that denies their religiously based practices, their religious freedom would be violated and the diversity we claim to value would be reduced.

As this book progresses, we will develop more fully our vision of religious freedom for all and the reasons for our present concerns. We will point a way forward that fully takes into account the true nature of religion as beliefs the faithful follow not only as members of religious congregations and as private individuals but also as citizens active in the public life of the nation. As we move in that direction, our vision of a nation marked by a renewal of religious freedom, pluralism, and tolerance will be realized.

2

When Religious Organizations Are Said Not to Be Religious

★

What if one morning you opened your favorite blog and read the headline, "Democratic Club May No Longer Require Its Leaders Be Democrats"? Most of us would conclude that the world had indeed gone mad. Yet on campus after campus, Christian student organizations are being denied official recognition and on-campus privileges because they have Christian belief and behavior standards for their members or leaders. And Christian humanitarian organizations have been challenged in court over policies to hire only persons who support their religiously shaped missions.

These situations have emerged out of the nondiscrimination laws our nation has rightly enacted to protect persons against discrimination in the form of exclusion from employment or membership in organizations. Persons may not be told to look elsewhere because of their race, ethnic background, religion, disabilities, gender, and—in some jurisdictions—sexual orientation.

No employer may hang out a sign reading, "No blacks need apply" or "No Catholics need apply."

This is good and proper. But nondiscrimination laws do raise some questions. May an on-campus sorority limit its membership to women and a fraternity to men? We have easily answered that question with a yes. We have also easily answered the question of whether a synagogue may only hire a Jew as its rabbi or an Episcopal church only an Episcopalian as its priest. But may laws forbidding discrimination based on religion prevent a faith-based organization that is not a religious congregation from limiting its members, leaders, or staff to persons in agreement with its religious beliefs? Differences of opinion, and at times bitter controversy, have arisen. Here we present case studies of two such instances.

Must a Christian Student Organization Admit Atheists?

San Diego State University recently withdrew official on-campus recognition from the Alpha Delta Chi sorority, an evangelical sorority, and from Alpha Gamma Omega-Epsilon, an evangelical fraternity, and stripped them of the privileges that all other on-campus student organizations possess. The problem according to the university was that these Christian student organizations were engaging in discrimination because they restricted their members to Christians in agreement with their statements of faith. The students took their case into the federal courts but lost on both the District Court and the Court of Appeals levels. The Supreme Court refused to hear their case.

Three crucial observations testify to the violation of religious freedom in this instance. One is that San Diego State University allows student organizations to impose belief or philosophical conditions on their members and leaders and still retain official university recognition. No one disputes this fact. Both the university and the decision by the United States Court of Appeals for the Ninth Circuit openly acknowledged that student organizations may restrict membership to those who support the group's purpose and "agree with the particular ideology, belief or philosophy the group seeks to promote." The court's decision went on to state, "For example, the Immigrant Rights Coalition requires members to 'hold the same values regarding immigrant rights as the organization.' The San Diego Socialists at San Diego State require students to be in 'agreement with our purpose.' The Hispanic Business Student Association opens membership to those 'who support the goals and objectives' of the organization."[1] The net result of this policy is—as it was expressed in a brief filed before the Supreme Court asking it to review this decision—that the university's policy "allows Democrats to bar Republican leaders, Vegans to bar hunters, African-Americans to bar white supremacists, but not Christians to bar atheists."[2]

This is deeply troubling. It has the effect of discriminating against Christian and other religiously based student groups. Belonging to a religious tradition involves holding to certain beliefs and certain perspectives on the world and how to live one's life in the world. In that sense it is akin to holding to certain political or philosophical beliefs. To grant on-campus recognition and the privileges that go with that recognition to those holding secular

"The net result of this selective policy [of San Diego State University] is therefore to marginalize in the life of the institution those activities, practices and discourses that are religiously based. While those who espouse other causes may control their membership and come together for mutual support, others, including those exercising one of our most fundamental liberties—the right to free exercise of one's religion—cannot, at least on equal terms."[3] —Judge Kenneth Ripple, in his concurring opinion in *Alpha Delta Chi-Delta Chapter v. Reed*.

beliefs and perspectives but to deny them to those holding religiously based beliefs and perspectives is a clear instance of discrimination against religious student organizations.

A second observation is based on San Diego State University's very public commitment of encouraging diversity on campus. Its website has a separate tab labeled "Diversity" that proudly proclaims "Diversity Starts Here."[4] But at San Diego State, diversity ends at religion. The university fails to see that its policy of not recognizing religious student organizations works against diversity. It, in effect, says we welcome and encourage racial, ethnic, sexual orientation, and gender diversity but not religious diversity.

The goal of any university's commendable push for greater diversity on campus is not simply having isolated individuals of differing racial, ethnic, economic, sexual orientation, or gender backgrounds enrolled in the university. Instead, the goal of diversity necessarily involves persons of differing backgrounds being able to band together in order to gain mutual support and encouragement, to make their voices heard, and to be recognized as part of the university community. As already seen, one of the Court of Appeals judges acknowledged that San Diego State University's policy "marginalize[d] in the life of the institution" evangelical Christians and other religious groups by refusing their organizations on-campus privileges that other student organizations are given.[5] The university thereby violated its own stated goal of greater on-campus diversity.

It is important to note that deeply committed religious students on a state university campus—and this is especially true of evangelical students—can sometimes feel they are in a minority position. A recent nationwide study of college and university faculty by the Institute for Jewish and Community Research found that of all religious groups, evangelicals elicited the most negative feelings by faculty members. Some "53% [of faculty] said that they have cool/unfavorable feelings toward evangelical Christians. Faculty feelings about evangelicals are significantly cooler than any other religious group. . . . These negative feelings are noted across academic disciplines and demographic factors."[6]

It is not surprising, therefore, that evangelical and other deeply religious students on secular university campuses at times may feel they are in a marginalized position similar to other historically marginalized groups, such as racial and ethnic minorities, gays and lesbians, and the physically disabled. Yet, while San Diego State University encourages and makes allowance for certain students to band together to better express themselves and their beliefs, it actively discourages and sends off campus organizations based on religion. As Tish Warren, a staff member for InterVarsity Christian Fellowship, a national association of Christian student organizations, has asked, "Do we want different communities with conflicting narratives and ideologies to be authentically represented on campus or not?"[7] San Diego State has clearly answered "No" in the case of religiously based narratives and ideologies.

A third observation notes that the Court of Appeals' decision stated that the Christian student groups are still "free to express any message they wish, and may include or exclude members on whatever basis they like; they simply cannot oblige the university to subsidize them [by on-campus recognition] as they do so."[8] This is true, of course. What is also true, however, is that other student organizations *can* receive advantages that go with on-campus recognition, such as "access to campus office space and meeting rooms, free publicity in school publications, and participation in various special university events."[9] Meanwhile, religiously based student organizations are denied these same benefits officially recognized student groups receive. Religious student organizations are thereby put at a disadvantage compared to secular-based student organizations. Religions and religious groups are free to do what they want, but they must stick to their own private world. They must function without the benefits other, nonreligious student

> "If common sense dictates that sororities should not be compelled to select male leaders (and it does), ought not RSOs [Religious Student Organizations] (whether Buddhist, Muslim, Jewish, Sikh, Humanist, or Christian) have a similar right to choose student leaders that reflect their religious missions?"[10]—Alec Hill, president of InterVarsity Christian Fellowship

groups receive, such as on-campus meeting rooms and use of campus communications. This most definitely is not consistent with full religious freedom.

One final note: the situation at San Diego State University is anything but unique. In 2014 the entire California State University system with its nineteen campuses enforced a policy that now requires all on-campus, recognized student groups to accept all students as potential leaders, whether or not they agree—in the case of a religious student organization—with the religious basis and mission of the organization. As a result all the InterVarsity Christian Fellowship student groups on these campuses, as well as other religious student groups, now must operate without the advantages that go with official recognition. Vanderbilt University, the Hastings School of Law, Rollins College, the University of Michigan at Dearborn, Rutgers University, the University of North Carolina, and Tufts University have all refused to recognize and grant on-campus status to Christian student organizations or have threatened to do so. InterVarsity Christian Fellowship counted some forty campuses as of 2012 where their chapters have been threatened with derecognition because of religious standards for their leaders.[11]

It takes no great insight to recognize that if an organization—whether an environmental, LGBT, political, or religious organization—cannot require its members, and surely its leaders, to adhere to the beliefs around which it is organized, that organization faces the prospect of losing its distinctiveness and thereby its reason for existing. This is no minor matter.

Can a Humanitarian Organization Also Be a Religious Organization?

World Vision is a large international relief and development agency. Its United States affiliate has an annual budget of $1 billion. Speaking of its international partnerships, Nicholas Kristof, a *New York Times* columnist, has described its size: "World Vision now has 40,000 staff members in nearly 100 countries. That's more staff members than CARE, Save the Children and the worldwide operations of the United States Agency for International Development [USAID]—combined."[12]

World Vision (U.S.) is also a deeply Christian agency in the evangelical tradition. Its website testifies to its Christian commitment: "World Vision is a Christian humanitarian organization dedicated to working with children, families, and their communities worldwide to reach their full potential by tackling the causes of poverty and injustice. . . . Motivated by our faith in Jesus Christ, we serve alongside the poor and oppressed as a demonstration of God's unconditional love for all people."[13] Similarly, Steven McFarland, vice president and chief legal officer for World Vision (U.S.), has stated, "Our faith is very important; our mission is very important. . . . It is who we are, the power of God working through our people. We are not just another humanitarian organization, but a branch of the body of Christ."[14]

Because its mission is clearly rooted in its religious faith, World Vision requires its employees to indicate their agreement with its statement of faith when first employed and to reaffirm this faith commitment each year. In 2006 three of its employees said they were no longer in agreement with this statement of faith. World Vision, after counseling with them, concluded it had no choice but to let these three employees go. The next year these employees brought suit, charging religious discrimination in employment, a practice generally barred for nonreligious employers by federal law.[15] World Vision countered that because it is a religious organization, it is exempt under the law from legal bars to hiring and firing decisions based on religion. The Supreme Court had upheld the exemption of religious organizations from the law that banned employment decisions based on religion in 1987.[16] In 2010 the United States Court of Appeals for the Ninth Circuit decided in a split two-to-one decision that World Vision is indeed a religious organization and was therefore exempt under the law. It could legally dismiss the three employees.

World Vision and the right of faith-based organizations to make hiring decisions based on religion prevailed. The freedom of faith-based organizations to hire staff who are in agreement with their religious views and beliefs was protected. But two sobering facts remain. First, the hiring rights of faith-based organizations was protected only after a lengthy and expensive court battle and by a narrow two-to-one margin. If one of the two majority judges had ruled differently, World Vision would have lost. Religious freedom was protected but only by the narrowest of margins.

Second, the reasoning put forward by the dissenting judge, Judge Marsha Berzon, is deeply troubling. She essentially argued that since World Vision is not a church engaging in prayer and worship-like activities, it must be a nonreligious, humanitarian organization engaging in secular activities. At one point in her dissenting opinion she argued that the determining factor in deciding whether World Vision and other similar faith-based organizations

"As Christians, we have a mandate and calling from God to this work, and I think this higher calling makes a difference in everything World Vision does."[17] —Eric W., a World Vision employee

are truly religious is that "we ask *only* whether the primary activity of a purportedly religious organizations consists of voluntary gathering for prayer and religious learning."[18] Later she wrote, "The vast majority of World Vision's work consists of humanitarian relief, including . . . providing potable water, emergency medical care, and vocational training to refugees and vulnerable populations throughout the world. . . . World Vision's purpose and daily operations are defined by a wide range of humanitarian aid that is, on its face, secular. . . . In short, World Vision is nothing like a church."[19]

This sort of reasoning is anything but the fringe thinking of an extremist jurist. It is closer to the mainstream thinking in our nation's leading universities and major media outlets. It is embraced by many judges. We will come across this thinking many times in this book. It views religion as limited to churches and other religious congregations and the prayers, rituals, and celebrations conducted in them for and by their members. That is "religion." Acts of love and mercy done in the name of and in obedience to the commands of one's faith are "secular" activities. According to this view, organizations the faithful have created in order to carry out their religious duties do not have religious freedom rights. By this thinking World Vision, in spite of the deeply religious language in its mission statement and in spite of its own clear insistence that it is a religiously imbued organization, would be declared nonreligious.

But this cannot be. Recall the four quotations we cited in chapter 1, all of which made clear that the Christian religion requires acts of mercy and help to those in need. Doing so is a religious act. Thus, Mother Teresa, when she cared for the sick and dying in the name of Jesus Christ, was much more than a humanitarian worker engaged in a secular activity. She was living out the gospel of Jesus Christ as much as a priest celebrating the Eucharist. For Christians—and for adherents of many other faiths—acts of humanitarian assistance are faithful responses to demands God has placed on them, and that assistance must be given to all in need, not only to one's fellow believers. They are as much the fulfillment of one's religious duties as prayer and worship.

In addition, there is another way in which humanitarian acts are, for the faithful, religious acts and the organizations formed to enable them to fulfill their religious obligations are religious organizations. A faith-based organization's religious faith shapes *how* it goes about fulfilling its religious duties. A Catholic hospital, for example, is dedicated to healing the sick, but its religious faith prevents it from "healing" a troubled pregnancy by way of abortion. An evangelical and a thoroughly secular counseling center—even though equally committed to helping the drug or alcohol dependent—may very well take somewhat different approaches to helping those who come to them. Loma Linda University Medical Center, a Seventh-Day Adventist hospital, declares as its mission, "To continue the teaching and healing ministry of Jesus Christ." And it describes as its vision: "Innovating excellence in Christ-centered health care."[20] Is "Christ-centered" health care identical to secular health care? Clearly Loma Linda does not think so.

It is hard to think of a religious freedom violation more serious than a government edict that tells a Christian, Jewish, or Muslim organization it cannot hire persons who share in and are committed to its religious mission. If that happens, that organization will virtually cease to exist as a faith-based organization. For a Hassidic Jewish organization—or for other Orthodox Jewish organizations—to have to hire Christians, Muslims, or gentile unbelievers would destroy that organization as an organization with a distinctive religious tradition and engaged in distinctive practices rooted in that tradition.

It is hard to disagree with the well-known University of Virginia legal scholar Douglas Laycock when he states, "Nothing—nothing—is more important to religious identity than the ability to hire employees who actually support the religious mission and will faithfully execute it."[21]

> "A religious organization cannot answer a divine calling without freedom to define itself and its doctrine, polity, and personnel."[22]
> —From a legal brief filed by the Christian Legal Society in *Spencer, Hulse, and Youngberg v. World Vision*

We all quickly recognize the truth of this position when it comes to churches, synagogues, mosques, and temples. As we noted earlier, no one argues that the Catholic Church should be forced to hire Protestants as priests or evangelical churches to hire unbelievers as their pastors. But in the minds of many, things change when it comes to an organization such as World Vision. Implicitly, many assume it is a nonreligious or only a vaguely religious organization, not an organization firmly rooted in the evangelical tradition. Going back to the reasoning of the dissenting judge in the World Vision case, she was convinced that World Vision and other similar faith-based organizations helping those in need are merely humanitarian organizations engaging in secular activities. If this were the case, there would be no need for that organization to hire only persons who share its religious convictions. But, as we have seen, that most definitely is not the case. An organization can be deeply religious *and* deeply engaged in humanitarian work. For Christians, this is exactly what Jesus Christ commanded.

But what if a faith-based organization has accepted government funding for some of its activities? Many believe it then forfeits any right it may have had to take into account the religious beliefs of prospective employees. Faith-based organizations that do so are labeled as engaging in unlawful discrimination. The head of the advocacy organization Americans United for the Separation of Church and State once wrote in a statement that is probably more revealing than he intended, "If government pays for a social work position, every qualified applicant should be considered for the job regardless of their views on religion."[23] This statement is revealing because it erroneously assumes that whether an applicant for a position in a religious organization is "qualified" for that position has nothing to do with that person's religious views. But whether job applicants at a religiously based organization support that organization's religious mission is highly relevant in determining their qualifications. Just as one's views on the environment are highly relevant to a person applying for a job at an environmental protection organization, so also one's religious views and beliefs are highly relevant to a person applying for a job at a religiously based organization.

That is not changed when government helps fund the work an organization is doing in the community. To claim otherwise is to argue that faith-based organizations must choose between accepting government funding or keeping their religious character. In effect, this would penalize religiously based organizations that desire to keep their religious character, since they would be denied funds that other organizations engaged in similar, parallel activities are receiving. To penalize an effective, capable organization because it wishes to keep its religious faith is the very definition of a violation of religious freedom.

The two case studies we have presented in this chapter—that of San Diego State University denying official recognition to student religious organizations and the challenge to World Vision's ability to have only employees who support its religious beliefs and mission—both concern faith-based organizations and their ability to maintain their distinctive religious character. Central to that ability is the freedom of a faith-based organization to insist that those who comprise it support its religious goals and purposes.

One final note is that different faith-based organizations will differ on the importance for them and their identity to have members, leaders, or employees in agreement with their religious beliefs and standards. Some believe it is important that its leaders be in religious agreement but will welcome members and staff with different religious beliefs. Others will believe it important that all its employees be in agreement with its religious beliefs. Faith-based organizations also differ on how they define being in religious agreement. Rarely in the Christian tradition do faith-based organizations believe it important their members or staff belong to one certain church or denomination. What *is* important is that the faith-based organizations themselves be free to decide what religious standards to insist upon and to whom in their organizations to apply them. That is crucial in order for a faith-based organization to maintain its distinctive nature and identity.

The Wrong Kind of Christian

TISH HARRISON WARREN

I thought I was an acceptable kind of evangelical.[1] I'm not a fundamentalist. My friends and I enjoy art, alcohol, and cultural engagement. We avoid spiritual clichés and buzzwords. We value authenticity, study, racial reconciliation, and social and environmental justice.

Being a Christian made me somewhat weird in my urban, progressive context, but despite some clear differences, I held a lot in common with unbelieving friends. We could disagree about truth, spirituality, and morality, and remain on the best of terms. The failures of the church often made me more uncomfortable than those in the broader culture.

Then, two years ago, the student organization I worked for at Vanderbilt University got kicked off campus for being the wrong kind of Christians.

In May 2011, Vanderbilt's director of religious life told me that the group I'd helped lead for two years, Graduate Christian Fellowship—a chapter of InterVarsity Christian Fellowship—was on probation. We had

---

1. This essay first appeared in the September 2014 issue of *Christianity Today*. Used by permission of the author and *Christianity Today*, Carol Stream, IL 60188.

to drop the requirement that student leaders affirm our doctrinal and purpose statement, or we would lose our status as a registered student organization.

I met with him to understand the change. During the previous school year, a Christian fraternity had expelled several students for violating their behavior policy. One student said he was ousted because he is gay. Vanderbilt responded by forbidding any belief standards for those wanting to join or lead any campus group.

In writing, the new policy refers only to constitutionally protected classes (race, religion, sexual identity, and so on), but Vanderbilt publicly adopted an "all comers policy," which meant that no student could be excluded from a leadership post on ideological grounds. College Republicans must allow Democrats to seek office; the environmental group had to welcome climate-change skeptics; and a leader of a religious group could not be dismissed if she renounced faith midyear. (The administration granted an exception to sororities and fraternities.)

Like most campus groups, InterVarsity welcomes anyone as a member. But it asks key student leaders—the executive council and small group leaders—to affirm its doctrinal statement, which outlines broad Christian orthodoxy and does not mention sexual conduct specifically. But the university saw belief statements themselves as suspect. Any belief—particularly those about the authority of Scripture or the church—could potentially constrain sexual activity or identity. So what began as a concern about sexuality and pluralism quickly became a conversation about whether robustly religious communities would be allowed on campus.

In effect, the new policy privileged certain belief groups and forbade all others. Religious organizations were welcome as long as they were malleable—as long as their leaders didn't need to profess anything in particular; as long as they could be governed by sheer democracy and adjust to popular mores or trends; as long as they didn't prioritize theological stability. Creedal statements were allowed, but as an accessory, a historic document, or a suggested guideline. They could not have binding authority to shape or govern the teaching and practices of a campus religious community.

At first I thought this was all a misunderstanding that could be sorted out between reasonable parties. If I could explain to the administration that doctrinal statements are an important part of religious expression—an ancient, enduring practice that would be a given for respected thinkers like Thomas Aquinas—then surely they'd see that creedal communities are intellectually valid and permissible. If we could show that we weren't homophobic culture warriors but friendly, thoughtful evangelicals committed to a diverse, flourishing campus, then the administration and religious groups could find common ground.

When I met with the assistant dean of students, she welcomed me warmly and seemed surprised that my group would be affected by the new policy. I told her I was a woman in the ordination process, that my husband was a PhD candidate in Vanderbilt's religion department, and that we loved the university. There was an air of hope that we could work things out.

Line in the Sand

But as I met with other administrators, the tone began to change. The word *discrimination* began to be used—a lot—specifically in regard to creedal requirements. It was lobbed like a grenade to end all argument. Administrators compared Christian students to 1960s segregationists. I once mustered courage to ask them if they truly thought it was fair to equate racial prejudice with asking Bible study leaders to affirm the resurrection. The vice chancellor replied, "Creedal discrimination is still discrimination."

Feeling battered, I talked with my InterVarsity supervisor. He responded with a wry smile. "But we're moderates!" We thought we were nuanced and reasonable. The university seemed to think of us as a threat.

For me, it was revolutionary, a reorientation of my place in the university and in culture.

I began to realize that inside the church, the territory between Augustine of Hippo and Jerry Falwell seems vast, and miles lie between Ron Sider and Pat Robertson. But in the eyes of the university (and much of the press), subscribers to broad Christian orthodoxy occupy the same square foot of cultural space.

The line between good and evil was drawn by two issues: creedal belief and sexual expression. If religious groups required set truths or limited sexual autonomy, they were bad—not just wrong but evil, narrow-minded, and too dangerous to be tolerated on campus.

It didn't matter to them if we were politically or racially diverse, if we cared about the environment or built Habitat homes. It didn't matter if our students were top in their fields and some of the kindest, most thoughtful, most compassionate leaders on campus. There was a line in the sand, and we fell on the wrong side of it.

My husband and I love the idea of the university, a place of libraries and lawns, a space set aside to grapple with the most vital questions of truth, where many different voices gather to engage in respectful conversation. Both of us had invested considerable time and money into pursuing advanced degrees. He was preparing to be a professor.

We liked being in pluralistic settings, mining for truth in Nietzsche and St. Benedict alike. But if Christian orthodoxy was anathema in this purportedly broad-minded university, where did that leave us? What did that mean for our place in the world and how we interacted with culture?

And what did that mean for all the PhD candidates in my student group who were preparing for a life of service in the secular university? Did we need to take a slightly more Amish route of cultural engagement?

And what did all this mean for the university?

Facing an Impasse

A culture of fear seemed to be growing on campus. There were power plays and spin. A group of professors penned a thoughtful critique of the new policy but remained silent when sympathetic department heads warned that going public could be "career damaging."

As a private university, Vanderbilt had the right to adopt particular beliefs and exclude certain religious groups. What bothered me was that they didn't own up to what they were doing. I wanted them to be truthful, to say in their brochure, "If you are a creedal religious person, don't expect to find a campus group here." I wanted intellectual honesty and transparency about their presuppositions.

Instead, top officials seemed blind to their assumptions, insisting all religious groups were welcome while gutting our ability to preserve defining beliefs and practices.

Those of us opposed to the new policy met with everyone we could to plead our case and seek compromise. We published essays and held silent protests with signs calling for pluralism and religious liberty. Hundreds of students and some faculty respectfully objected to the new policy. Catholic and Protestant students, low-church and high-church, met together daily in front of the administration building to pray.

As a writer and pastor, I value words, love careful argument, and believe good ideas prevail. I believed that if we cast a vision of principled pluralism, showed how value-laden presuppositions are inherent in any worldview, and reiterated our commitment to Vanderbilt and avoided the culture wars, the administration would relent.

But as spring semester ended, fourteen campus religious communities—comprising about 1,400 Catholic, evangelical, and Mormon students—lost their organizational status.

A year later, my family and I moved to a different state to plant a new InterVarsity chapter. It was painful to leave beloved faculty, students, and ministry colleagues with the campus conflict unresolved. There was no happy ending, no triumphant reconciling moment. After that long and disorienting year, I left not in confident, defiant protest, but in sadness. What I thought was a misunderstanding turned out to be an impasse.

We Are Here

What's happening at Vanderbilt is happening at other universities. Increasingly, orthodox beliefs and practices are forbidden as those in power forfeit a robust understanding of religious pluralism.

Our task moving forward is to resist bitterness, cynicism, or retalia-
tion, demonizing the university or the culture. As Aleksandr Solzhenitsyn
said, the line between good and evil runs through every human heart,
a reality that makes everything more complex. We have to forgive and
to look squarely at places in our own heart that require repentance. In
community, we must develop the craft of being both bold and irenic,
truthful and humble.

While we grieve rejection, we should not be shocked or ashamed by
it. That probationary year unearthed a hidden assumption that I could be
nuanced or articulate or culturally engaged or compassionate enough
to make the gospel more acceptable to my neighbors. But that belief is
prideful. From its earliest days, the gospel has been both a comfort and
an offense.

N. T. Wright points out in *Paul: In Fresh Perspective* that the unlikely
message of a crucified Jew raised from the dead "was bound to cause
hoots of derision, and, if Acts is to be believed, sometimes did." Throughout history and even now, Christians in many parts of the world face
not only rejection but violent brutality. What they face is incomparably
worse than anything we experience on United States college campuses,
yet they tutor us in compassion, courage, and subversive faithfulness.

We need not be afraid; the gospel is as unstoppable as it is unacceptable. Paul persisted, proclaiming that Jesus was, in fact, the world's true
Lord. And, as Wright notes, "people (to their great surprise, no doubt)
found this announcement making itself at home in their minds and hearts,
generating the belief that it was true, and transforming their lives with a
strange new presence and power."

After we lost our registered status, our organization was excluded
from new student activity fairs. So our student leaders decided to make
T-shirts to let others know about our group. Because we were no longer
allowed to use Vanderbilt's name, we struggled to convey that we were a
community of Vanderbilt students who met near campus. So the students
decided to write a simple phrase on the shirts: *We are here.*

And they are. They're still there in labs and classrooms, researching
languages and robotics, reflecting God's creativity through the arts and

seeking cures for cancer. They are still loving their neighbors, praying, struggling, and rejoicing. You can find them proclaiming the gospel in word and deed, in daily ordinariness. Though it is more difficult than it was a few years ago, ministry continues on campus, often on the margins and just outside the gates. God is still beautifully at work. And his mercy is relentless.

Tish Harrison Warren is a priest in the Anglican Church in North America and works with InterVarsity at the University of Texas–Austin.

3

When Laws and Religious
Convictions Clash

★

Few today would dispute James Madison's justly famous words, "The Religion then of every man must be left to the conviction and conscience of every man; and it is the right of every man to exercise it as these may dictate. This right is in its nature an unalienable right."[1] Indeed, forcing a faith-based organization to violate its religious convictions sounds more like a totalitarian than a democratic regime.

Yet organizations deeply rooted in religious traditions are today increasingly finding themselves in a position where laws and government regulations are forcing or pressuring them to act contrary to long-held religious beliefs. Most of these are faith-based nonprofit organizations, but there are also some for-profit businesses whose owners have infused them with sincerely held religious principles and who are now being pressured to act contrary to those principles. In this chapter we present case studies of four incidents where religiously based nonprofit organizations have been pressured to violate their religious convictions. In the next chapter, we present a case study of a for-profit business that is having the same experience. These case studies relate actual, documented happenings; they are not hypothetical or future possibilities. Nor are they, unfortunately, rare exceptions.

Arizona, Alabama, and Undocumented Immigrants

In 2010 the Arizona legislature passed and its governor signed a law that, among other things, made it a crime to "transport or move or attempt to transport or move an [undocumented] alien in this state in a means of transportation" and to "harbor" an undocumented alien in "any building."[2] The law raised many legal issues and ignited a firestorm of controversy.

Among the issues this law raised was a serious religious freedom issue. A brief filed before the Supreme Court by the United States Conference of Catholic Bishops, which was joined by mainline Lutheran and Presbyterian churches, declared that the Arizona law "presents a serious threat to religious liberty."[3] What was the religious freedom violation these church bodies saw? The brief went on to explain, "Forcing Catholic institutions to check the papers of all they serve (and turn away undocumented immigrants) would . . . fundamentally violate the Catholic Church's religious beliefs that it cannot turn away others in need."[4] Earlier the brief had made clear the religious beliefs the law was requiring Catholic institutions, under threat of criminal charges, to violate: "The Catholic Church, like others, believes that it has a moral and religious duty to serve all in need. That is an important religious tenet flowing directly from Scripture. . . . The Church believes that it must follow Jesus's command concerning these migrants: 'Amen, I say to you, whatever you did for one of these least brothers of mine, you did for me.'"[5]

The law made illegal what many faith-based organizations' religious beliefs required. It was against the law for a church organization to find undocumented immigrants in the desert who could be near death—many of whom were victims of unscrupulous "coyotes" (persons who lead others across the border for high fees)— and transport them to a church-run shelter and provide them with food and water. Nor could Catholic Charities or other faith-based organization legally provide food to the needy without turning away the hungry who were undocumented. It would have to turn away from an overnight shelter women and their children in desperate need if they were undocumented. The law demanded faith-based organizations violate deeply held, religiously based beliefs.

One can argue back and forth about United States immigration laws and their enforcement. Opinions understandably vary. But when faced with immediate and urgent human needs—such as a hungry father desperately seeking food for his family, a vulnerable mother and her children seeking the safety and warmth of an overnight shelter, or young children wandering the deserts without water and facing death—many faith-based groups believe they are compelled by their religious beliefs to offer the desperately needed help. In the hungry father, the homeless mother, and the young children in dire need, they see Jesus Christ himself as the one in need. Yet the Arizona government was telling them they could be prosecuted for following the clear commands of their faith. The law and religious convictions clashed.

Arizona has not been alone in posing such dilemmas to persons and organizations of faith. In 2011 Alabama passed a law that

"We do not wish to stand before God and, when God asks if we fed the hungry or clothed the naked to reply: yes, Lord, as long as you had the proper documents."[6] —The Reverend Robert J. Baker, Bishop of Birmingham

made it "unlawful for a person to . . . harbor or shield . . . an [undocumented] alien from detection in any place in this state, including any building or any means of transportation."[7] The Reverend Robert Baker, the Catholic bishop of Birmingham, reacted in a letter to the members of his diocese, a letter in which other clergy joined. It stated that in Alabama,

> The law prohibits almost every activity of our Catholic Social Services. If it involves an undocumented immigrant, it is illegal to give the disabled person a ride to the doctor; give food or clothing or financial assistance in an emergency; allow them to shop at our thrift stores or to learn English; it is illegal to counsel a mother who has a problem pregnancy, or to help her with baby food or diapers thus making it far more likely that she will choose abortion. This law attacks our very understanding of what it means to be a Christian.[8]

The federal court system has largely blocked both the Arizona and Alabama laws from going into effect. In 2012 the Supreme Court held most of the provisions of the Arizona law to be unconstitutional, and in 2012 the United States Circuit Court of Appeals for the Eleventh Circuit did the same for the Alabama law. The federal government argued, and the courts largely agreed, that federal immigration law preempted these state laws' attempts to deal with the problem of illegal immigration. However, one searches the courts' written opinions in vain in these cases for any reference to the religious freedom concerns various religious groups had raised in court filings.[9] There may be good legal reasons for the courts not to have done so, but it is unfortunate that these concerns were not addressed.

Even though these laws never fully went into effect, they nevertheless serve as illustrations of how laws can be enacted that forbid faith-based organizations to do what their religious faith requires.

Adoption and Foster Care Agencies in Illinois

For forty years Catholic Charities affiliates in Illinois had served, as the *New York Times* put it, "as a major link in the state's social service network for poor and neglected children."[10] The Evangelical Child and Family Agency had also provided child and family services since 1946. For some forty years, Illinois largely depended upon these and other private, nonprofit family and child care agencies—not state agencies—to provide foster care for abused and neglected children and for adoption services. The state granted yearly contracts to these nonprofit agencies to provide these services; the nonprofit agencies hired staff and developed the needed facilities. This arrangement worked to the benefit of the agencies, needy children and families, and the State of Illinois. The faith-based agencies could offer services to more children and families they felt God had called them to serve. And the needy children and families could receive excellent services from local agencies with caring staff members. The state benefited because the faith-based agencies relieved it of a burdensome task and supplemented state-provided funds with their own money and volunteers.

But this seemingly win-win-win situation was recently thrown into turmoil when the State of Illinois suddenly required the Catholic and evangelical agencies to act in violation of their deeply held religious beliefs or face the termination of their funding. The issue was that of adoption and foster care by unmarried couples, whether heterosexual or same-sex couples. The Catholic and evangelical agencies are rooted in religious traditions that believe unmarried cohabitation and same-sex relationships are against God's will and intentions for humankind. One can agree or disagree with this stance; no one can dispute this is a sincere, long-held, religiously based position that has been thoughtfully reached.

The problem began in 2010 when the Illinois legislature passed the "Illinois Religious Freedom Protection and Civil Union Act." It made possible civil unions for same-sex couples that carried with them essentially the same legal rights and obligations as marriage. After this act passed, the Illinois Department of Children and Family Services informed all the private agencies with whom they were contracting for adoption and foster care services that in the future they would be required to place foster care and adoptive children with same-sex couples and cohabiting heterosexual couples on the same basis as they did married households. If they refused to do so, the state would no longer contract with them for family and child care services, no matter how long the state had been contracting with them and no matter how effective their services had been. Illinois thereby pressured the Catholic Charities and evangelical agencies to change long-standing practices rooted in their faiths' understanding of the God-established nature of marriage and the family. The faith-based agencies suddenly faced a cruel dilemma: either violate their long-held religious beliefs or refuse state money and be unable to serve thousands of needy children and families.

The Catholic Charities family-service agencies in four dioceses went to court, claiming the violation of their religious freedom rights. They pointed out that the 2010 "Illinois Religious Freedom Protection and Civil Union Act" that the Department of Children and Family Services was citing as a basis for not renewing their contracts, proclaimed in its title its commitment to religious freedom. Also, Section 15 of the law in its very first sentence specifically states, "Nothing in this Act shall interfere with or regulate the religious practice of any religious body."[11] In addition, the legal complaint filed by Catholic Charities cited a revealing exchange about this section's religious freedom protections when the law was moving through the legislature between one of the senators, Senator William Haine, and the law's chief sponsor, Senator David Koehler.

> Senator Haine referred to a variety of religious practices on the part of "these institutions of faith of all denominations, Christian and Jewish [which] go to their various agencies providing *social*

services, retreats, religious camps, homeless shelters, senior care centers, *adoption agencies*, hospitals, a wide gamut of things. So, that's covered under the first sentence" of Section 15, he queried, to which Senator Koehler answered: "Yes."[12]

The Evangelical Child and Family Agency filed a brief in support of the Catholic Charities agencies. It appealed to the Illinois Religious Freedom Restoration Act, which prohibits government from unnecessarily placing a substantial burden on the free exercise of religion. It argued that by refusing to renew the state's contracts with the Catholic Charities agencies, the State of Illinois pressured the agencies "to engage in conduct forbidden by their faith [which] undeniably imposes a substantial burden on their religious exercise."[13]

It appeared that Catholic Charities had a strong legal case. Nevertheless, on August 18, 2011, John Schmidt, an Illinois Circuit Court judge, ruled in a brief, three-page opinion against Catholic Charities. Most troubling, he based his ruling on the narrow, technical question of whether the Catholic Charities agencies had a property interest in the renewal of their contracts to provide child welfare services. Unfortunately, he never considered the strong religious freedom claims raised by Catholic Charities and the Evangelical Child and Family Agency. The religious freedom rights of faith-based organizations that had provided faithful service to the families and children of Illinois for many decades in response to the commands of their faith did not enter into his decision. Since 2011 Illinois legislators have introduced bills that would clearly spell out the religious freedom rights of faith-based organizations not to place children with same-sex or unmarried heterosexual couples, provided that they inform such couples of other agencies that would accept them for foster care or adoption services. These bills, however, have never made it out of committee.

As a result, the affected faith-based agencies faced the cruel choice of either violating their religious faith or ending programs their faith had called them to offer to needy children and their families. The Catholic Charities agencies and the Evangelical Child and Family Agency both decided they had no choice but to stop providing the foster care and family services the state had helped fund for the past forty years. The Evangelical Child and Family Agency transferred 242 children and 185 families they were helping to nearby secular agencies. The Catholic Charities agencies did the same for almost two thousand children who were in foster care under their supervision.[14] They now carry on privately funded but truncated foster care, adoption, and family service programs.

One final note to this sad story. The result was most definitely not in the interest of needy children, as the Illinois Department of Children and Families claimed. It is a clear case of the clash between certain attitudes currently in ascendancy and religious freedom. No one should pretend it is anything else. Under the prior system, same-sex or cohabiting heterosexual couples could adopt children or provide foster care since there were public and private agencies willing to place children with them. In fact, the faith-based agencies involved regularly referred unmarried couples (whether same-sex or heterosexual) to other agencies willing to place children with them. No one was being denied the opportunity to adopt a child or provide foster care to a child; no needy child was being denied care. The agencies involved in this case were not trying to stop other agencies from placing children with unmarried couples; they only did not want to be required to do

"The Catholic Church has successfully partnered with the state for half a century in providing foster care and adoption services. . . . The losers will be the children, foster care families and adoptive parents who will no longer have the option of Catholic, faith-based services."[15] —A joint statement by Bishop Thomas John Paprocki of Springfield and other bishops whose dioceses were affected

so themselves. The bills proposed in the Illinois legislature that would protect the right of faith-based agencies not to place children with unmarried couples explicitly require such agencies to refer unmarried couples to other agencies willing to place children with them. Yet these bills, as noted earlier, have never even been brought to a vote in the legislature.

The chief effect of Illinois' action was to disrupt established relationships with case workers and caregivers for hundreds of children and families and to reduce the number of agencies providing foster care and adoption services. It was the needy children who suffered. Hundreds of children receiving foster care through Catholic Charities agencies in four cities, who had already experienced turmoil and disruption in their lives, experienced further uncertainty. Also, there was less diversity in the agencies providing foster care and adoption services. Those families desiring family services from Catholic or evangelical agencies no longer had that choice. In addition, Ken Withrow, director of the Evangelical Child and Family Agency, pointed out, "What's lost is a resource in the faith community of faith-based agencies, which may have an impact on the number of dedicated, compassionate, mission-driven types of families to take care of these kids."[16]

This story from Illinois is not unique. Faith-based child care agencies in Boston; San Francisco; and Washington, DC, have faced similar pressures on their right to follow their religious beliefs. These violations of religious freedom are not isolated, random instances where justice has gone awry. Unfortunately, there is a pattern here. And should the Supreme Court decide same-sex couples have a constitutional right to marriage, these pressures will grow even greater.

Faith-Based Universities and Government Mandates

Some may think football is at the heart of the University of Notre Dame. But the university itself has declared otherwise.

Faith is at the heart of Notre Dame's educational mission. . . .
Notre Dame embraces the richness of the Catholic intellectual
tradition, "consecrat[ing] itself without reserve to the cause of
truth." It aims to provide a forum where, through free inquiry
and open discussion, the various lines of Catholic thought may
intersect with the arts, sciences, and every other area of human
scholarship.[17]

Similarly, Wheaton College (Illinois) declares on its website,
"Committed to the principle that truth is revealed by God through
Christ . . . [Wheaton College's] curricular approach is designed
to combine faith and learning in order to produce a biblical perspective needed to relate Christian experience to the demands of
those needs."[18]

Both of these institutions—one in the Roman Catholic tradition
and one in the evangelical Protestant tradition—are religiously
based institutions rooted in their respective religious traditions.
And both institutions are currently in court seeking judicial protection from being forced by a government regulation to go against
their religiously based beliefs. This is another instance of laws
and religious convictions clashing.

The story goes back to August 2011 when the Obama administration's Department of Health and Human Services (HHS)
issued a regulation under the Affordable Care Act that required all
organizations with at least fifty employees, including faith-based
organizations, to offer contraceptive services free of charge in the

"A Catholic University's privileged task is to unite existentially
by intellectual effort two orders of reality that too frequently tend
to be placed in opposition as though they were antithetical: the
search for truth, and the certainty of already knowing the fount
of truth."[19] —Pope John Paul II in his Apostolic Constitution on
Catholic Universities

health care plans that cover their employees. Contraceptives were defined broadly enough to include certain drugs for which there is evidence they not only prevent conception but can cause the death of already fertilized eggs by preventing them from implanting in a women's uterus (the "morning after," or Plan B pill, and the "week after," or ella pill, and certain IUDs).[20] Thus, many see these drugs and devices as abortifacients, that is, as causing very early abortions. Those organizations that do not comply with the directive to offer all of the required contraceptives in their health insurance plans face heavy fines that, in the case of some entities, would run into millions of dollars a day.

This original HHS directive provided for a religious exemption for organizations whose consciences would forbid them from providing such services. However, the religious exemption was extremely narrow, applying only to an organization that could meet all four of the following criteria: (1) its purpose is the inculcation of religious values, (2) it primarily hires persons who share the organization's religious tenets, (3) it primarily serves persons who share those tenets, and (4) it is a religious congregation, an integrated auxiliary, or an association of religious congregations. The "integrated auxiliaries" to which the fourth criterion for exemption refers includes such entities as a religious congregation's community service program or a school run as a department of a congregation, not as an independent entity.

Thus the religious exemption was crafted to protect the religious freedom rights of religious congregations and their integrated auxiliaries but not religiously based health care, social service, and educational organizations, including religious colleges and universities such as Notre Dame and Wheaton. The religious exemption was rooted in the inaccurate view of religion as limited to religious congregations in their core religious practices and rituals conducted for their own members. This view does not see colleges and universities such as Notre Dame and Wheaton as being truly religious and engaged in religiously shaped activities—or,

"One of the ways America has fostered and protected [religious] diversity is by nurturing a robust understanding of religious liberty that includes granting certain exemptions to people who need them in order to be true to their religious faith. Religious exemptions protect people in situations where legislative or executive acts might otherwise unnecessarily force them to violate their consciences."[21] —Timothy George, professor of jurisprudence, Princeton University, and Hamza Yusuf, president, Zaytuna College

at the least, it regards them to be religious in a less than genuine or substantial manner. Yet both institutions have long histories of being embedded in their respective religious traditions. Both insist they in fact are religiously based.

Since the initial issuing of this regulation, HHS has backtracked numerous times. It first attempted to clarify that a community ministry run by a religious congregation would not be excluded by dropping the first three elements of the criteria an entity would have to meet to qualify for a religious exemption. But the exemption continues to apply only to religious congregations and activities directly under their control.

HHS also attempted to accommodate faith-based organizations other than the already exempt religious congregations by creating a new category of faith-based organizations, including institutions such as Notre Dame and Wheaton. Under the most recent of these iterations—issued in July 2014—faith-based organizations' employees would still have access to contraceptives, IUDs, and Plan B and ella drugs free of charge through their employers' health insurance plans, but it was claimed the costs would be borne not by the organizations themselves but by their insurers. In the case of self-insured entities, the organizations' agents who administer the self-insured plan would pay for the coverage.

This means HHS has created three categories of organizations in regard to its contraceptive mandate: (1) churches, other religious congregations, and their integrated auxiliaries, which are exempt from the mandate; (2) other nonprofit, faith-based organizations, which HHS has sought to accommodate by requiring their insurance companies or agents to provide the contraceptives; and (3) for-profit businesses, which are fully subject to the mandate even when infused with religiously based beliefs and values. (We will discuss faith-based for-profit businesses in the next chapter.)

Both Notre Dame and Wheaton fall into the second of these categories. They have, however, thus far rejected the compromise accommodations as not meeting their religiously based objections since they believe they are still complicit in providing their employees with the contraceptives to which they object, even if their funding of them is now indirect. They argue that the insurance companies will provide the contraceptives out of money the colleges have paid the companies in their premiums. In addition, even under the most recent version of the regulations they are still required to inform HHS of their religiously based objections to the provision of contraceptives or, in the case of Wheaton, in what it views as abortifacients. This then leads HHS to inform their insurance companies or agents of this fact, which is what triggers the insurance companies or agents to provide the disputed contraceptives free of charge.

The use of artificial contraceptives and abortifacients runs counter to long-held Catholic moral teachings. Evangelicals, as a rule, have no objection to contraception, but have long-standing, religiously based objections to Plan B and ella drugs and certain IUDs, which they view as abortifacients. Their objections do not rest on some suddenly discovered claim designed to avoid a new regulation.

Thus both Notre Dame and Wheaton brought suit in federal courts, claiming the HHS mandate unnecessarily requires them to do what their religion forbids. At the outset Notre Dame's lawsuit made clear this is an issue of being forced to violate long-standing religious beliefs, not an issue of the legality or availability of contraceptives. It states that its lawsuit "is not about whether people have a right to abortion-inducing drugs, sterilization, and contraception. Those services are, and will continue to be, freely available in the United States. . . . Through this lawsuit, Notre Dame does not seek to impose its religious beliefs on others."[22] The university's suit goes on to state that it "simply asks that the government not impose its values and policies on Notre Dame, in direct violation of its religious beliefs."[23]

The Wheaton College lawsuit described the religious freedom issue at stake similarly: "Wheaton will have to decide whether to obey the HHS mandate—which would force it to cover abortion-inducing drugs for free—or whether to obey its foundational religious beliefs. . . . The price of remaining faithful will be steep. . . . And yet the value of Wheaton's faith and integrity are incalculable. Wheaton faces an impossible choice."[24] It later makes clear that "Wheaton holds and follows traditional Christian beliefs about the sanctity of life. . . . Wheaton College therefore believes and teaches that abortion ends a human life and is a sin."[25] Its complaint goes on to make clear that its concern is not the general availability of drugs it views as abortifacients; its concern is with it being forced to be involved in providing them to its employees. Its complaint points out that the government has "a host of obvious alternatives for furthering its interest in expanding contraceptive access. Any of these alternatives would avoid any need to conscript religious objectors into providing these drugs and services against their consciences."[26]

Both the Notre Dame and Wheaton lawsuits are still pending in federal courts. Notre Dame was denied an injunction against having to comply with the regulation while its case wends its way through the courts. In late 2013 Notre Dame complied with the required paperwork that resulted in their employees receiving contraceptive coverage in their health insurance even while complaining strenuously and continuing its case in the courts. In early 2014 the United States Court of Appeals for the Seventh Circuit, in a split two-to-one decision, upheld a lower court decision not to grant immediate relief to Notre Dame. But in March 2015 the Supreme Court ordered the Court of Appeals to reconsider its decision not to grant Notre Dame immediate relief. In July 2014, the Supreme Court granted Wheaton College an injunction that temporarily relieved it of the need to file the paperwork to which it objected.[27]

The final outcome is yet to be decided by the courts. In both the Notre Dame and Wheaton cases, litigation continues. And, as noted earlier, the HHS regulations that mandate contraceptive coverage as they apply to faith-based nonprofit organizations keep evolving. Meanwhile, the religious freedom rights of Notre Dame and Wheaton remain in limbo. They continue under the threat of being forced by law to be involved in the provision of health services that their religiously based convictions forbid.

Notre Dame and Wheaton are not alone. Some ninety nonprofit, religiously based organizations, both Catholic and evangelical, have filed lawsuits claiming the HHS mandate forces them to violate deeply held religious beliefs. These include thirty-seven colleges and universities, forty faith-based charities, and fifteen dioceses.[28] Most of these cases are making their way through the courts. One can agree or disagree with the religiously based, moral stance these organizations are taking; no one can doubt the sincerity of their objections or the seriousness of the religious freedom issue the HHS mandate has raised.

The underlying problem that has led to seemingly endless litigation and HHS's continuing efforts to find a way to accommodate faith-based organizations is the failure of HHS to simply grant faith-based nonprofit organizations an exemption from its contraceptive mandate. This is what it has done for religious congregations and activities under their direct control. The University of Notre Dame, Wheaton College, and a host of other faith-based organizations currently in court over the contraceptive mandate are assumed to be less than fully religious. Thus their religious freedom is thought to be less in need of protection as compared to religious congregations and their integrated auxiliaries.

Government Grants and Religious Beliefs

Since 2006 the United States Conference of Catholic Bishops (USCCB) had received annual grants from the HHS to provide help to victims of human trafficking, many of whom were women who had been forced into prostitution and held as no better than slaves.[29] The USCCB did not provide these services directly but found and subcontracted with direct-service agencies that provided the actual services. In doing so it assured help to those who are truly among the most vulnerable and needy of human beings. In 2011 it applied for a renewal of its grant. As was normal, career officials and an independent review board in HHS oversaw the grant competition. Based on past performance, they ranked the USCCB at or near the top among the grant applicants. Nevertheless, the $4.5 million in grant money was given to three other applicants, two of which had "scored significantly below the Catholic bishops' application by the review panel."[30] News reports confirmed the review board had "ranked the Catholic groups far above other applicants."[31]

Meanwhile, the Massachusetts chapter of the American Civil Liberties Union (ACLU) filed suit against HHS for its previous grants to the Catholic bishops for their efforts on behalf of victims of human trafficking. In 2012 the judge ruled in favor of the ACLU and held that HHS had violated the Constitution in making grants to the Catholic bishops for assisting victims of human trafficking.[32]

What was going on here? Why would anyone object to an organization using government grants to support exemplary services to victims of human trafficking? The problem lay in the bishops' insistence—in keeping with long-standing Catholic teaching—that their subcontractors not provide abortion or contraceptive services to the victims of human trafficking. The top officials in HHS—who overruled their own staff's recommendations—decided that the grants should only be made to organizations willing to provide or make referrals for abortion and contraceptive services. The ACLU argued—and the District Court judge agreed—it was an unconstitutional establishment of religion for HHS to make grants to organizations that, on religious grounds, did not provide certain services.

We thus come across another instance where a faith-based organization faced pressure to limit or give up its faith-based practices. There is a religious freedom problem when faith-based organizations are denied government contracts or grants to provide important public services because they hold to certain religiously rooted beliefs and practices. As Sister Mary Ann Walsh of the USCCB said, "In the hierarchy of needs for trafficking victims, it would seem that safety, food, shelter, legal support, and medical care [ought to] have priority."[33]

Denying grants or contracts to certain faith-based organizations would be understandable, if those organizations' religiously-rooted beliefs and practices meant they were providing inferior services as compared to other organizations. As already seen, that was not the case here. Program reviews by HHS staffers had ranked the Catholic bishops' program highly in comparison to other applicants for funds. In fact, the Justice Department lawyers had argued in the lawsuit brought by the ACLU that the bishops had been "resoundingly successful in increasing assistance to victims of human trafficking."[34]

The judge in the case brought by the ACLU of Massachusetts, however, decided that allowing a grant recipient to follow certain religiously rooted practices constituted an unconstitutional establishment of religion. He reasoned that when HHS makes grants to nonprofit organizations, those organizations become

"All faith-based service providers are threatened, because the court's novel rule severely restricts the ability of government to accommodate any contractor's religious commitments, Catholic or otherwise. The people most in need of human services—the poor, the sick, the marginalized—would suffer the most from such a broad exclusion of faith-based providers from cooperation with government."[35] —The Reverend William Lori, Archbishop of Baltimore, and the Reverend Jose Gomez, Archbishop of Los Angeles, commenting on the judge's decision in *ACLU of Massachusetts v. USCCB, Sebelius, and Sheldon*

agents of the government—that is, the government has delegated to them the authority to make certain decisions. He went on to reason that since it would be unconstitutional for a government agency to impose religiously based standards, it was unconstitutional for the Catholic bishops to do so. In his view the Catholic bishops' policy on abortion and contraceptives had become the government's policy. He wrote that HHS "delegated authority to a religious organization to impose religiously based restrictions on the expenditure of taxpayer funds, and thereby impliedly endorsed the religious beliefs of the USCCB and the Catholic Church."[36] The fact that the Catholic bishops' opposition to abortion and contraceptives "was motivated by deeply held religious beliefs" was no protection from their being discriminated against in the awarding of grants.[37] That fact actually *required* the government to do so. The judge held that since the Catholic bishops had become agents of the government, making decisions the government had authorized them to make, they could no more impose religiously motivated standards than the government itself could. Holding to certain religious beliefs and practices made a faith-based organization ineligible for grants nonreligious organizations could receive. Being religious became a liability or a disadvantage.

But this ought not to be. When a faith-based organization receives a grant from government to help it provide certain important public services, it does not become an extension or agent of the government. Its actions do not become government actions. This is a key point we cannot emphasize too strongly.

When government insists it will not make grants to some faith-based organizations due to certain of their religiously based beliefs and practices—even though, as here, they are not interfering with the effectiveness of the services being funded—government is clearly discriminating against those faith-based organizations. There is a clear religious freedom problem whenever government offers millions of dollars to faith-based groups if only they will give up some of their religiously based beliefs and practices. On pain of losing government grants and contracts, faith-based organizations are told they must go against their religious beliefs. Meanwhile, secular organizations of a parallel or similar nature are, of course, free to pursue government contracts and grants with no need to change their policies or practices. The end result is to favor secular organizations over faith-based ones, not because of the greater effectiveness of the services the secular organizations are providing but because of certain religiously based practices the faith-based organizations' beliefs compel them to follow.

As is true with the other three case studies considered in this chapter, this instance of the USCCB and its loss of a government grant is not an isolated case. In fact, more faith-based organizations may very well face similar pressures in the future. One source of pressure may be the executive order President Obama issued in 2014 that requires all organizations with whom the federal government contracts not to discriminate against persons in their hiring based on their sexual orientation or gender identity.[38]

Many faith-based organizations and their leaders had petitioned the White House prior to its release of this executive order to include strong exemption language for faith-based organizations with a religiously based conduct standard that restricts sexual relations to man-woman marriage. The Obama administration failed to do so, although it did retain an existing rule that faith-based contractors may consider religion when deciding whom to hire.

How will this executive order affect faith-based organizations? This will not be clear for some time. Most faith-based organizations that receive federal money for their programs do so in the form of grants, not contracts, and thus will not be directly affected by it. More important, it remains to be seen how the administration, and the courts, will interpret that religious hiring exemption that remains valid. Will a faith-based organization's employee conduct standards be permitted, as part of its protected religious hiring right—as we believe they should—or will they be forbidden because of the new prohibition of discrimination on the basis of sexual orientation?

But this 2014 executive order—and the White House's failure to include language that fully protects faith-based organizations—creates potential religious freedom problems for faith-based organizations that offer the exact services and products the federal government seeks to purchase by means of contracts. Simply because of their religiously based employee conduct codes they could be excluded from receiving government contracts, just as the USCCB has been excluded from receiving a federal grant to help victims of sex trafficking because of its commitment to Catholic moral teaching on abortion and birth control. Pressure would thereby be put on them to water down or abandon entirely their religiously based standards. If this happens, their religious freedom would be narrowed and limited, and the ability of faith-based organizations to contribute fully to the good of others in our society would be undermined.

4

Can a For-Profit Business Have a Religious Conscience?

★

In the eyes of the law, can there be such a thing as a faith-based for-profit business? Can a for-profit business, or even a large corporation such as Exxon, have religious freedom rights? At first glance many assume it is absurd to say that for-profit businesses have religious freedom rights. As one commentator wrote, "Corporations do not have bodies or souls, do not worship, do not get baptized or bar mitzvahed, and do not bend their knee in prayer."[1] But, as is often the case in the real world, when one takes a closer look, things turn out not to be so simple. In this chapter we present a case study of a for-profit company that in fact is faith-based and had to fight all the way to the Supreme Court to protect its religious freedom.

Hobby Lobby

Hobby Lobby is a for-profit corporation with more than five hundred arts and crafts stores in forty-one states, 13,000 full-time employees, and annual sales of some $5 billion. It is a family corporation, owned by the Green family of Oklahoma City.[2] The Greens are evangelical Christians who seek, as reported in the *New York Times*, to run their "company on biblical principles, including closing on Sunday so employees can be with their families, paying nearly double the minimum wage and providing employees with comprehensive health insurance."[3] The director of a Christian ministry and friend of the Greens has described how they view their religious and business lives: "They don't see their secular and their spiritual life as bifurcated. They see it as intertwined."[4] Hobby Lobby's mission statement makes clear its religious foundation.

> In order to effectively serve our owners, employees, and customers the Board of Directors is committed to:
>
> - Honoring the Lord in all we do by operating the company in a manner consistent with biblical principles.
> - Offering our customers an exceptional selection and value.
> - Serving our employees and their families by establishing a work environment and company policies that build character, strengthen individuals, and nurture families.
> - Providing a return on the owners' investment, sharing the Lord's blessings with our employees, and investing in our community.
> - We believe that it is by God's grace and provision that Hobby Lobby has endured. He has been faithful in the past, we trust Him for our future.[5]

As evangelical Protestants, the Greens have no objection to the use of contraceptives and have long provided for them in their employees' health plan. But as evangelicals they have religiously based objections to providing their employees with four of the twenty forms of birth control measures approved by the FDA: two types of drugs (Plan B and ella) and two types of IUDs (intra-uterine devices), for which there is evidence they may not operate

> "We believe wholeheartedly that it is by God's grace and provision that Hobby Lobby has been successful. We simply cannot abandon our religious beliefs to comply with this mandate."[6]
> —David Green, Hobby Lobby founder and CEO, on the HHS contraceptive mandate

by preventing conception but by preventing an already fertilized egg from developing.[7] The Greens, along with many others, view them as abortifacients.

As seen in the prior chapter, faith-based colleges and universities such as the University of Notre Dame and Wheaton College hold to similar views and as a result are in court defending their right not to be forced into violating their religious convictions. (Notre Dame, as one would expect of a Catholic institution, has religiously based objections to all contraceptives, whereas Wheaton, as an evangelical institution, only has objections to the same drugs and devices as Hobby Lobby did.) Hobby Lobby and the Green family faced the same pressures since they too fell under the 2011 regulations of the HHS that required them to provide contraceptive coverage—broadly defined to include IUDs and Plan B and ella drugs—in Hobby Lobby's health insurance plan. In fact, the pressures to go against their beliefs were even stronger since HHS made no attempt to accommodate the religiously based beliefs of the owners of for-profit firms. The Greens therefore faced fines of $100 a day for each employee not covered by the forms of birth control to which they had religiously based objections. Since Hobby Lobby has some 13,000 employees, these fines would have come to some $1.3 million per day, or $475 million a year. On the other hand, if Hobby Lobby and the Green family opted to avoid paying for the coverage to which they had religiously based objections by providing no health insurance coverage at all, they would have been fined $26 million per year.

Plus they would have still been forced into violating their faith by leaving their employees without the health insurance that they, because of their faith, had been providing for them for years. The Greens faced the choice either to violate their religious beliefs or face fines that could put them out of business. This was no minor matter.

In 2012 Hobby Lobby and the Green family filed a lawsuit against the HHS regulations asking for an injunction, asserting their "religious beliefs prohibit them from deliberately providing insurance coverage for prescription drugs or devices inconsistent with their faith, in particular abortion causing drugs and devices. Hobby Lobby's insurance policies have long explicitly excluded—consistent with their religious beliefs—contraceptive devices that might cause abortions and pregnancy termination drugs like RU-486."[8] They claimed they "face an unconscionable choice: either violate the law, or violate their faith."[9] HHS acknowledged, "The Greens' sincerely held religious opposition to certain forms of contraception is not subject to question."[10]

Hobby Lobby appealed not only to First Amendment free exercise protections but also to the 1993 Religious Freedom Restoration Act (RFRA). This act provides that laws may not "substantially burden" the free exercise of religion. There is only an exception if two conditions are met: a substantial burden on a person's free exercise of religion must be needed in order to further what is termed a "compelling government interest," and the means used must be the least restrictive of religious freedom. Only when these conditions are met may the law infringe on individuals' and organizations' practice of their sincerely held religious beliefs. RFRA thereby creates strong, though certainly not absolute, protections against the federal government interfering with persons' practice of their religious beliefs. In the case of the Green family and Hobby Lobby, however, HHS argued in court that RFRA applies only to individuals and nonprofit organizations, not to for-profit businesses such as Hobby Lobby.

The key question the *Hobby Lobby* case therefore raised was this: Does a for-profit business, whether incorporated or unincorporated, enjoy constitutional or other legal religious freedom protections when its owners seek to operate their business in accordance with their deeply rooted religious beliefs?

After losing at the District Court level, the United States Court of Appeals for the Tenth Circuit ruled in favor of the Greens, holding that Hobby Lobby was likely to prevail in its lawsuit and sent the case back to the District Court.[11] The District Court issued a preliminary injunction suspending the enforcement of the HHS mandate until a final judicial decision would be reached in the case. The Supreme Court agreed to hear this case, along with a similar case involving a business owned by a Mennonite family with religious freedom objections similar to those of the Green family. In 2014 the Supreme Court held by a narrow five-to-four margin in favor of Hobby Lobby and the Green family. Hobby Lobby therefore does not have to provide in its employees' health insurance plan the four types of birth control means to which its owners objected on religious grounds.

The Supreme Court majority applied RFRA and held, first, that it applies to closely held, family owned corporations such as Hobby Lobby. The Court logically stated,

> An established body of law specifies the rights and obligations of the *people* . . . who are associated with a corporation in one way or another. When rights, whether constitutional or statutory, are extended to corporations, the purpose is to protect the rights of these people. . . . And protecting the free-exercise rights of corporations like Hobby Lobby . . . protects the religious liberty of the humans who own and control those companies.[12]

The Court then went on to apply RFRA and held that even if one accepts that the contraceptive mandate as applied to Hobby Lobby furthered a compelling governmental interest, the mandate did not do so by the least restrictive means available. It held there were less restrictive means—means less constricting of the Greens' religious freedom—by which the government could ensure the Hobby Lobby employees would receive free of charge the four birth control measures to which the Greens had religious objections. For example, the Court suggested the government itself could provide them, or the government could provide for-profit companies such as Hobby Lobby the same sort of accommodation it was already providing faith-based, nonprofit organizations (as we saw in chap. 3). The Court thereby ruled the religious freedom rights of Hobby Lobby and the Green family had been violated, and they did not have to provide the four challenged birth control drugs or devices. The religious freedom rights of the Green family, as they engaged in a for-profit business, were thereby protected. Religious freedom prevailed.

But the protection of the religious freedom of faith-based for-profit businesses nonetheless remains on shaky ground. There is still reason for concern. For one thing, the Supreme Court decision on the question of whether the contraceptive mandate furthered a compelling interest by the least restrictive means was a very close five-to-four decision. If only one justice in the majority had reached a different conclusion, the decision would have gone against the Greens. In addition, the reasoning used by the four dissenting justices and by many prominent commentators following the decision is deeply troubling. The dissenting opinion, written by Justice Ruth Bader Ginsburg, stated that surely the Greens themselves may choose not to make use of the challenged birth control measures, but "that choice may not be imposed on employees who hold other beliefs."[13] Many commentators made the same point in even stronger language. In an editorial titled "The Justices Endorse Imposing Religion on Employees," the New York Times editorialized that "denying women access to full health benefits is discrimination."[14] Two writers for the liberal think tank the Center for American Progress asserted, "Today's

Supreme Court decision gives for-profit corporations . . . the right to impose a burden on their workers by coercing them to adhere to religious beliefs that are not their own."[15]

These, and many other reactions to the *Hobby Lobby* decision, frame it in an inaccurate, highly prejudicial manner. This worries us deeply. Hobby Lobby and the Green family were not—and the Supreme Court did not approve—imposing their religious beliefs onto others, denying women access to health care, or coercing women to adhere to religious beliefs not their own. This would have been the case only if Hobby Lobby had tried to force their employees not to use the four birth control measures to which it had objections by, for example, firing any employees they discovered were using them. Or one might be able to talk about an effort to impose religious beliefs on others if the Greens were lobbying Congress to pass legislation making it unlawful for women to use these forms of birth control. But that was not the case. The only true coercion in this case involved those who were seeking to force the Green family to act contrary to their religious beliefs.

Admittedly, the employees of Hobby Lobby who wished to use one of the four means of birth control to which the Greens have religious objections will now be put to some added expense or inconvenience unless or until the government devises some other means to make them available free of charge. But that is far different than prohibiting access to those forms of birth control. What is truly at issue here is what we as a society value more: the religious freedom rights of deeply religious persons and the businesses they have founded or the ability of their employees to obtain birth control free of charge. Especially given other means by which government policies can make birth control freely available, we clearly believe the sincerely held religious freedom rights of persons and their businesses should take precedence.

Digging a bit deeper, there also seems to be a hidden assumption behind many of the expressions of dismay over the *Hobby Lobby* decision. Two of the commentators we quoted earlier also referred

"Free exercise [of religion] implicates more than just freedom of belief. It means, too, the right to express those beliefs and to establish one's religious (or nonreligious) self-definition in the political, civic, and economic life of our larger community."[16] — Justice Anthony Kennedy in his concurring opinion in the *Hobby Lobby* case

to "allowing the religious beliefs of the owners of for-profit, *secular* corporations to be used as justification to deny their employees the contraceptive health coverage that they are entitled to."[17] But on what basis can they conclude that Hobby Lobby is a nonreligious, secular business, even while the owners themselves, their mission statement, and their faith-inspired practices all indicate it is a business deeply rooted in its owners' religious beliefs? A clue can be found in the quotation we cited at the beginning of this chapter that insisted corporations do not have religious freedom rights since they "do not have bodies or souls, do not worship, do not get baptized or bar mitzvahed, and do not bend their knee in prayer." But the same could be said of *any* incorporated entity, including even churches. In addition, even when an entity does not look or act like a church or synagogue, it does not mean they cannot be religious. As we have seen earlier, religion is more than worship, and freedom of religion is more than freedom of worship. This is a basic theme to which we will return later.

Faith-Based For-Profit Businesses

The *Hobby Lobby* case—and other similar cases we could cite—teach there indeed are faith-based for-profit businesses. The assumption that a business cannot be faith-based and guided by religious principles cannot be correct. Another example is

Pomegranate Supermarket in Brooklyn, New York, which sells only kosher food and has been hailed as a sign of the resurgence of Orthodox and Hasidic Judaism. *New York Times* columnist David Brooks observes, "For the people who shop at Pomegranate, the collective covenant with God is the primary reality and obedience to the [moral] laws is the primary obligation."[18] The same could be said of its owners. The owners of Hobby Lobby and Pomegranate Supermarket come from different religious traditions, but they are united in seeking to live out their faiths in the businesses they run.

Also, it is not at all uncommon for businesses to be run in keeping with the owners' moral concerns or standards. Some coffeehouses proclaim their commitment to using only "fair trade" coffee. During the apartheid era in South Africa some businesses divested themselves of South African holdings or investments out of conscience as a way of bringing pressure to bear on the white minority government. Some mutual funds proclaim themselves as socially responsible funds, refusing to invest in tobacco companies or certain military industries, and favoring "green" companies over heavy polluters. Similarly, the ice-cream maker Ben and Jerry's is a publicly traded company, and yet, far from seeking

> "Many religions impose, and at least some businesses follow, religious requirements for the conduct of profit-making businesses. Thus businesses can be observed to engage in actions that are obviously motivated by religious beliefs: from preparing food according to ancient Jewish religious laws, to seeking out loans that comply with Islamic legal requirements, to encouraging people to 'know Jesus Christ as Lord and Savior.' These actions easily qualify as exercises of religion."[19] —Mark Renzi, professor, Catholic University of America School of Law and Senior Counsel, the Becket Fund for Religious Liberty

simply to make money, it devotes a part of its profit to several social and political causes, including the promotion of same-sex marriage. It has now restructured itself as a B corporation, "a new type of corporation that uses the power of business to solve social and environmental problems," as it proudly states.[20] These are all examples of companies seeking to run their businesses in keeping with certain moral values and beliefs. In so doing, they are acting in the best tradition of moral pluralism and freedom to support causes they believe will lead to a better world. Many people believe our nation would be better off if more business owners infused them with moral values and goals beyond turning the largest profit possible.

The frequent infusion of businesses with moral concerns leads to the following observation: If it is appropriate, and even commendable, for businesses to be run in keeping with certain moral commitments of their owners, it is hard to object to businesses being run in keeping with certain religiously based moral commitments.[21] For many, their moral commitments—their beliefs in what is right and wrong—are rooted in their religious faith. On what possible basis can we as a society commend and support businesses that seek to follow certain moral values based in nonreligious commitments but stifle and limit businesses that follow certain religiously based moral values? Justice Samuel

"The simple truth is that if we want businesses, incorporated or not, to be responsible for their actions, they must be treated as having some moral agency. And with moral agency and accountability must go the freedom to act in accordance with conscience. If we want the Greens' businesses and other businesses like them to act conscientiously, they must have the freedom to follow their consciences."[22] —Mary Ann Glendon, professor, Harvard Law School

Alito made this point in the Court's opinion in its *Hobby Lobby* decision.

> For-profit corporations, with ownership approval, support a wide variety of charitable causes, and it is not at all uncommon for such corporations to further humanitarian and other altruistic objects. Many examples come readily to mind. . . . If for-profit corporations may pursue such worthy objectives, there is no apparent reason why they may not further religious objectives as well.[23]

This means that when business owners run their businesses according to certain religious standards, attempts to require those businesses to ignore or violate those religious standards raise important religious freedom questions. Those questions cannot be dismissed simply because for-profit businesses are involved.[24]

In addition, for religious freedom purposes two frequently made distinctions are more apparent than real. Yet they are often used to claim for-profit businesses should not be given religious freedom protections. One of these distinctions is the for-profit versus nonprofit distinction. The government in the *Hobby Lobby* case admitted that RFRA and its religious freedom protections apply to faith-based nonprofit organizations. But it claimed they did not apply to Hobby Lobby because it is a for-profit business.

For religious freedom purposes, however, the nonprofit versus for-profit distinction is a less real distinction than is often assumed. It is one made by the Internal Revenue Service to determine an organization's tax status. It does not rest on a fundamental difference in the nature of entities. For example, there could be a nonprofit neighborhood health clinic run by Catholic Charities that contains a pharmacy that dispenses certain drugs. Elsewhere in the same city there could be a for-profit drugstore owned by a devout Catholic family. In response to the faith of its owner, it often makes vital drugs available at low or no cost to low-income persons who otherwise could not afford them, much like the faith-based nonprofit health clinic does. If a municipal edict would require both pharmacies to dispense all FDA-approved contraceptives, both pharmacies would likely have religiously based objections. Yet if religious freedom protections apply to nonprofit organizations and not to for-profit organizations, one pharmacy would have a basis to assert its religious freedom rights and the other would not. In instances such as this, the nonprofit versus for-profit distinction is one without a substantive difference.

Real life examples abound. Crossway Books and Tyndale House Publishers are two evangelical publishing houses with large lists of books with a Christian orientation. They are very similar in their mission statements and goals.[25] Yet one is organized as a nonprofit firm and the other as a for-profit firm. It is hard to think of a reason why one should have religious freedom protections and the other not.

The distinction with a difference is between organizations— whether nonprofit or for-profit—that are rooted in certain sincerely held, clearly articulated religious convictions and organizations that are not. If ever the argument would prevail that the religious freedom protections of RFRA and the First Amendment apply to nonprofit but not to for-profit organizations—even when their religious commitments are similar—the religious freedom of faith-based for-profit firms would be in jeopardy.

A second distinction that is often made is between incorporated businesses versus unincorporated businesses, such as partnerships or sole proprietorships. But again, for religious freedom purposes this distinction is largely irrelevant. The brief filed by Hobby Lobby in its case before the Supreme Court used an example to make this point.

> The government agrees that a Jewish *individual* could exercise religion while operating a kosher butcher shop as a sole proprietor. Presumably, he could continue to exercise religion if he formed a general partnership with his brother. But the government says the

ability of this religiously observant butcher to exercise his faith abruptly ends—and the government's power to override his faith begins—at the moment of incorporation, even though he engages in the exact same activities as before.[26]

Many persons, when they think of incorporated businesses, think of huge corporations such as General Motors and Apple whose stock is publicly traded. But there are also what are called "closely held" corporations, whose stock is owned by a limited number of individuals and is normally not sold on stock exchanges. Their owners are often personally and directly involved in the business and its activities. For these business owners to infuse their businesses with religiously based values, beliefs, and moral standards is far from rare. Hobby Lobby and the Green family is an example of a closely held corporation, a fact the Supreme Court noted in its decision in support of their religious freedom claims.

But Hobby Lobby is not unique. There are other instances of for-profit businesses whose owners have deeply held religious beliefs that affect the way they run their businesses. They are vulnerable to having their religiously rooted practices challenged. Individual wedding photographers have been brought into court when their religiously rooted consciences have led them to decline photographing same-sex weddings or commitment ceremonies, even when there were other photographers available who would be happy for the business.[27] "There have been more than a half-dozen other instances of business owners, most citing their understanding of Christian faith, declining to provide services for same-sex weddings."[28] In 2015 the Supreme Court accepted a case that raises the question of whether or not same-sex couples have a constitutionally guaranteed right to marriage. If it decides that they do, more providers of wedding services who have religiously based objections to participating in same-sex weddings will face challenges to their religious freedom.

In addition, pharmacists have been threatened with the loss of their licenses because their religiously informed consciences did not permit them to dispense "morning after" and "week after" drugs. Some forty-seven for-profit businesses, both large and small, are in court seeking protection for their religious freedom. Their owners have religiously based objections to the 2011 HHS mandate requiring them to provide contraceptive coverage—broadly defined by HHS—in their employees' health plans.

On the other hand, we do not wish to overstate the number of faith-based for-profit businesses. One can spend hours on the internet looking up the mission statements of for-profit businesses and not find one with a mission statement with clear, explicit religious commitments such as are in Hobby Lobby's mission statement. Since religious freedom is a basic, crucial right, it is important to protect the religious freedom of faith-based for-profit businesses when and where they exist, but the proportion of such businesses is small and doing so will not involve widespread or huge numbers of businesses.

Limitations on Businesses' Religious Freedom Rights

In describing Hobby Lobby's position, one think tank described it as "the beginning of a blanket exemption to discrimination in the name of religion."[29] This is a fear others have voiced. Justice Ginsburg, in her dissenting opinion in the *Hobby Lobby* case, asked, "Where is the stopping point?"[30] She then went on to ask what would happen if an employer had religious objections to paying the legally required minimum wage, or paying women equal pay for equal work, or providing health care coverage for blood transfusions, antidepressants, or vaccinations.[31] Others have asked what would happen if an employer claimed religiously based racist beliefs for refusing to hire persons of color. What is to prevent for-profit firms from in fact doing what some have falsely claimed was going on in the *Hobby Lobby* case? "Hobby Lobby and other for-profit corporations are using a religious liberty argument to avoid complying with a government law they do not like."[32]

To be clear on the religious freedom rights of for-profit companies for which we are advocating, it is important to emphasize two limitations. Together they prevent extreme outcomes such as those that some commentators claim will occur. First, the for-profit firm must have a clear, explicit, demonstrable religious commitment. A credible religious commitment or belief cannot be created simply as a pretext for avoiding a law "they do not like." Courts have long quickly dismissed religious freedom claims that are not sincere but have suddenly sprung into being to avoid some legal requirement. Courts can look at mission statements, long-established practices, and roots in a known religious tradition to judge the sincerity of a firm's claimed religious beliefs. Courts would rightly be suspicious of a religious exemption claim based on religious beliefs that conveniently would allow the business to avoid a legal requirement to which it objects but affects the business in no other way. If a business is truly faith based, one would expect its faith commitments to be seen in a number of practices.

Second, neither the Supreme Court's *Hobby Lobby* decision nor the provisions of RFRA grant businesses a general right to avoid legal requirements to which they have religiously based objections. Both the Court's decision and RFRA itself are based on a weighing or balancing process. RFRA only grants a business the opportunity to make an argument about how vital its asserted religious claim is. On the one hand, the government must be able to demonstrate that the challenged legal requirement furthers a "compelling" government interest and that there is no other, less invasive, means for it to achieve that "compelling" interest. On the other hand, the business must be able to demonstrate that having to follow the legal requirement it is challenging would "substantially burden" its religious beliefs and practices. There must be more than just an inconvenience. In other words, RFRA sets up a twofold balancing process in which the good the public policy is intended to achieve is weighed against the burden it would impose on the religious objector, and the means by which the policy seeks to achieve that public good is weighed against other possible means of achieving that public good. RFRA provides no guarantee a business objecting to a legal requirement on religious grounds will win in the courts. It most definitely does not release companies simply to do whatever they desire.[33]

Most of the highly hypothetical abuses of RFRA and the Hobby Lobby decision that have been suggested can be answered by the need for any religious claim to be clearly sincere and by the balancing process RFRA establishes. Courts will not, and should not, protect racially discriminatory practices, unequal pay between women and men, avoidance of paying the minimum wage, and other such practices with clear benefits to the public interest. Nor are there any major religious traditions in the United States that insist on such practices. This in itself would cause any court to look very closely at the sincerity of any such religiously based exemptions a business might claim.

In summary, it is much too simple to suppose that for-profit firms cannot be faith based and have no basis to assert religious freedom claims. When government requires them to act contrary to their owners' deeply held religious beliefs, religious freedom is endangered in important ways. Hobby Lobby and the Green family—as well as other deeply religious owners of for-profit businesses—give testimony to this fact.

Religious Liberty Is about Who We Are

KRISTINA ARRIAGA DE BUCHOLZ

If you were to visit any of the thirty homes run by the Little Sisters of the Poor in the United States, you would find a clean and cheerful place where elderly people of all faiths spend the last days of their lives enjoying the loving embrace of caring nuns. Were it not for the Little Sisters, these elderly would otherwise be withering away in a government run home, a hospital, or even the streets, cast aside by their families and society, too sick and impoverished to afford costly end-of-life care.

The Little Sisters live out the foundational Christian command to care for the "least of these" in our society. They provide a service that no government could replicate, one that requires the lifelong, full-time commitment of the women who join their order. In 2009, Pope Benedict XVI canonized their foundress, Jeanne Jugan, and in doing so recognized the work of all of the women who have followed in her path. Less than two years later, however, these nuns received the startling news that according to the government they were not religious enough to qualify for a religious exemption from a new government regulation. Therefore, they would have to sign a form obligating their own insurer to pay for and provide in their health care plans drugs like Plan B birth control, an abortifacient, or face crippling fines.

For these women, whose religious vocation is protecting the dignity of all human life from conception until natural death, this was an unconscionable position to be put in. They could not provide the drugs and neither could they sign the form. For the Sisters signing constituted "formal cooperation with wrongdoing" which is not permissible within Catholic doctrine.

Many observers, even some Catholics, shrugged their shoulders and publicly encouraged the Sisters to sign the form. The Sisters would not. Instead they joined the wave of lawsuits against the government's Health and Human Services mandate, and their case was the first of the nonprofit cases to reach the Supreme Court. They are a client of the pro-bono religious liberty law firm that I manage, the Becket Fund for Religious Liberty. As I write this, their case is pending.

As a Cuban American, I am starkly aware of what a country looks like where religious groups like the Little Sisters of the Poor are shut down. It looks like this: rampant poverty and suffering. When the government pushes out of society the religious caretaker and pretends it can become one itself, it diminishes all freedoms. It is not only because the government cannot do this efficiently, it is because when it names itself the caretaker it also falsely claims to be itself the source of all rights. In 2014 a new wave of repression and beatings in Cuba plagued anyone who claimed that the government was not the source of all rights.

This kind of repression is one that Karol Wojtyla of Krakow, the future Pope John Paul II, observed in his native Poland. His own life experience inspired him to champion the Catholic Church's encyclical on religious liberty, *Dignitatis Humanae*. In 1967, the encyclical aptly articulated that the "human person is always to be taken as the primary consideration and the starting point for understanding religious freedom."

After three public debates, 126 speeches, and some six hundred written interventions, article 2 of Vatican II's final text on religious freedom asserted,

> The human person has a right to religious freedom. This freedom means that all men are to be immune from coercion on the part of the individuals or of social groups and of any human power . . . in matters religion no one is to be forced to act in a manner contrary to his own beliefs.
>
> Nor is anyone to be restrained from acting in accordance with his own beliefs, whether privately or publicly, whether alone or in association with others, within due limits.
>
> The Synod further declares that the right to religious freedom has its foundation in the *very dignity of the human person*. . . . This right of the person to religious freedom is to be recognized in the constitutional law whereby society is governed. Thus it is to become a civil right. (italics added)

In short, as the founder of the Becket Fund often stated, "Religious liberty is not an evangelistic tool. Religious liberty is not about who God is. Religious liberty is about who we are."

In America, the Catholic Church is the largest nongovernmental provider of health care, education, and charitable services to the poor. Catholic social workers, educators, and health care professionals help anyone in need, and do so without discrimination. In doing this, they are affirming that each human is born with dignity. This assertion of human dignity also recognizes a societal obligation.

In *Popularum progressio*, Pope Paul VI wrote, "Each man is also a member of society; hence he belongs to the community of man. It is not just certain individuals but all men who are called to further the development of human society as a whole." Pope Leo XIII emphasized that it is religion and especially religious institutions that carry out that work in society in *Rerum novarum*: "First of all, there is no intermediary more powerful than religion (whereof the Church is the interpreter and guardian) in drawing the rich and the working class together, by reminding each of its duties to the other, and especially of the obligations of justice." The command to care for the vulnerable has only been amplified by the current pope, Pope Francis, who has repeatedly called for a "poor church for the poor."

The right to freely exercise one's faith should be protected for all individuals, including those in the for-profit sector. Because like those motivated to do good in the nonprofit realm, countless Americans bring their faith values to the workplace, where their principles guide their moral decisions.

The Becket Fund also represented Hobby Lobby, a company founded by evangelical Christians who fought the same mandate as the Little Sisters all the way to the Supreme Court and won. While the media focused on the fact that its owners, David and Barbara Green, could not violate their faith and pay for employees' abortion-causing drugs, they often overlooked the fact that the same values that informed that decision also guided the Greens' decision to start full-time employees at double the minimum wage, to close their stores on Sundays, and to offer excellent health benefits including sixteen out of the twenty government-approved contraceptives the HHS mandate required under the Affordable Care Act. The press also largely ignored the fact that the Greens opposed only four of these drugs and devices because—as the government itself conceded—these four drugs could prevent implantation.

Society benefits when people of faith bring their values into the marketplace, whether it's for profit or not. However, a new claim is embedding itself in our society, one that eyes religion with suspicion and singles out people of faith.

That is why we at the Becket Fund for Religious Liberty have defended, as we like to say, the religious rights of people from "A to Z," from Anglicans to Zoroastrians. Religious freedom must include all religions and their adherents. It must also include nonprofit organizations, such as the Little Sisters of the Poor, the faithful have formed in response to their faith's demands, and enterprises, such as Hobby Lobby, that persons are seeking to run in keeping with their deeply held religious beliefs. As we strive toward better religious liberty jurisprudence, one that allows authentic pluralism to flourish, we as a society must rediscover gratitude for the essential role that religion plays in civil society. Our challenge is to restore this view of inherent dignity to society. Because religious liberty follows naturally from that view. And when religious liberty is not secure, nothing is.

....

Kristina Arriaga de Bucholz is the executive director of the Becket Fund for Religious Liberty. The views expressed in this essay are her own.

....

5

Common Threads

★

There is a puzzle in American society. Ask the average American in a poll if he or she values freedom of religion, and almost all will reply with a strong yes. But if Americans are fully committed to freedom of religion, why do we have the many violations of religious freedom illustrated by the case studies we presented in the prior chapters?

Some have argued these violations are due to irreligious persons, filled with hatred for all things religious, waging a war on religion. If this were the case, all we would need to do is rally persons of good will to beat back the attacks on religion. But we believe this is not the explanation for the puzzle—nor the proper response.

Others believe the religious freedom violations we have noted are random occurrences, examples of the occasional slipup in a system that otherwise is working well. They have faith in our constitutional system of checks and balances composed of courts, Congress, the executive branch, state and local governments, and a free marketplace of ideas. In time, these will lead to the needed corrections. We believe this also is not the answer. If it were, we would not need to write this book.

We are convinced something deeper and more troubling is at work. There are four threads composed of certain assumptions and beliefs prevalent in contemporary society in the United States. They connect the seemingly random, unrelated case studies we analyzed in the three previous chapters. Until we as a society recognize these threads and their errors, we will stumble from one religious freedom violation to another. To fully understand why all is not well with religious freedom, we need to understand these four threads that tie together the disparate religious freedom problems we have thus far documented.

Thread Number One: Freedom of Religion Is Equated with Freedom of Worship

The most fundamental, persistent thread tying together the various examples of religious freedom violations we have recounted is the assumption that all is well with religious freedom as long as religious congregations' worship services and individuals' private devotional activities are protected. Freedom of religion is thereby equated with freedom of worship. As long as churches, synagogues, mosques, and temples are protected in their right to conduct their religious celebrations and rituals in keeping with the tenets of their various faiths, and as long as

"Does our Constitution guarantee the freedom of religion, or does it merely allow a more limited freedom to worship? The difference is profound. Worship is an event. Religion is a way of life."[1] —Rick Warren, bestselling author and pastor of Saddleback Church, Lake Forest, California

families can worship God as they see fit in the privacy of their homes, what's the problem?

The problem is that Christianity and almost all other faiths believe the practice of their religion does not end with the prayers and worship services of the faithful. As we made clear earlier in chapter 1, integral to religious faith—that is, an inseparable, essential component of it—is the obligation to provide health care, education, and help to those in need. In addition, some business owners believe their faith calls them to run their businesses in keeping with certain faith-based values and beliefs. We cannot emphasize this comprehensive nature of religion enough, both because it is a fundamental fact of religious life and because it is often ignored—or its full implications are not understood.

And when Christians—or other believers—band together to create service organizations to fulfill their religious obligations more effectively than they could as individuals or as members of a local congregation, there is no reason why those organizations are any less religious than local congregations. In seeking to serve others, they are responding to the demands of their faith; they are acting in keeping with the tenets of their faith. Admittedly, they may be largely engaged in activities different from those carried out in worship services and within the walls of church buildings, but those activities are no less religious in nature.

One does not have to look far to find instances of the attitude that religion, and therefore freedom of religion, is limited to churches and other religious congregations. The case of World

"Any effort to confine religious people and their ideas to an innocuous spirituality or a merely ceremonial role in public life is a threat to religious liberty and to American democracy."[2] —Tim Shah and Tom Farr, Berkley Center for Religion, Peace and World Affairs, Georgetown University

Vision and its employment standards we recounted in chapter 2 is one such instance. Recall that the employees were let go because they were no longer in agreement with World Vision's statement of faith. They claimed discrimination in violation of the Civil Rights Act. On what basis? They insisted World Vision was a secular humanitarian agency, not a religious agency, and was thus not legally free to consider religious beliefs in their hiring practices.

The statement of one of the three Court of Appeals judges in this case that we cited in chapter 2 clearly reveals the presupposition that makes up this first thread: "The vast majority of World Vision's work consists of humanitarian relief, including . . . providing potable water, emergency medical care, and vocational training to refuges and vulnerable populations throughout the world. . . . World Vision's purpose and daily operations are defined by a wide range of humanitarian aid that is, on its face, secular. . . . In short, World Vision is nothing like a church."[3] The hidden assumption is that only institutions that resemble traditional churches—and we assume she would include other religious congregations—are truly religious. Ignored is the fact Christianity teaches that "providing potable water, emergency medical care, and vocational training to refuges and vulnerable populations" are as much religious acts as kneeling to receive the elements of the Eucharist or being submerged in the waters of baptism. Viewing religion as extending beyond worship to include acts of mercy toward others runs counter to beliefs and assumptions widespread in American society; it is also undeniable that this is what the Christian church teaches in most of its manifestations. As seen in chapter 1, Jesus Christ himself, popes, and other Christian leaders all testify to this fact. This is also true of other religious traditions.

Another example of this first thread can be seen in the Department of Health and Human Services' promulgation of its contraceptive mandate regulation in 2011. It recognized that some religious traditions—foremost among them the Catholic tradition—have long-standing, sincerely held objections to the use of contraceptives. Many in the evangelical tradition also have objections to the mandate since contraceptives were broadly defined to include what many believe are abortifacients. HHS therefore commendably exempted religious congregations and their integral auxiliaries from the mandate. But this exemption fell far short of what was needed to protect religious freedom because it was seemingly rooted in the assumption that religiously based health care, educational, and social service organizations are not truly religious in nature, or at the least not as fully religious as are churches and other religious congregations. Therefore, HHS apparently concluded they did not need to be exempt from its mandate.

In defending the requirement that contraceptive insurance coverage be provided by religiously based schools, health care organizations, and social service agencies, Dorothy Samuels, an editorial board member of the *New York Times*, wrote that "the provision of [contraceptive] preventive services without a co-pay does not interfere with a religious practice or ceremony. There is no impediment to the exercise of religion. . . . The rule does not interfere with church governance."[4] True, the contraceptive mandate does not interfere with any religious ceremonies nor with church governance. She is correct on that point. But that hardly settles the matter. Her conclusion that there is "no impediment to the exercise of religion" can only be true if "religion" is held not to speak to how religiously based organizations do the work God has called them to do. Samuels's unarticulated assumption is that religion and its duties are confined within the four walls of churches.

The fact that religiously conservative states such as Arizona and Alabama could enact laws that would forbid religious organizations from providing the care that undocumented immigrants desperately need—and that those organizations' faith demands they give—is an indication that these states did not see such acts of mercy as truly religious or truly demanded of many faith-based organizations' faiths. One cannot imagine either state forbidding the celebration of the mass, but no less an authority than the Pope has declared that celebration of the mass and acts of mercy to those in need are "inseparable" religious acts.[5]

A document put out by the liberal think tank Political Research Associates makes the same mistake. It declares at one point, "Note the generalization of 'religious liberty' rhetoric misstates the issue: No church has had to fight to maintain its religious freedoms."[6] It contends that churches' religious freedoms are intact, therefore there is no religious freedom problem. But this is only true if the religious freedom the Constitution and our laws protect are confined to churches and their activities.

Many of the violations of religious freedom we documented in earlier chapters are invisible if one begins with the false assumption that religion is only what takes place in churches and other religious congregations. What is needed is a recognition of the fact that religion and its practice are more than what takes place within religious congregations, and thus freedom of religion is more than the freedom of religious congregations to engage in religious rituals and celebrations. A change in an outlook that is widespread in American society is required.

A final observation serves as a sobering note for Christians, since they themselves may have contributed to this outlook. Caring for the needy has often not received the emphasis from them that the founder of Christianity and many of its most prominent leaders have given it. The Richard Stearns quotation in chapter 1 insisting the demands of Christianity are not met by worship and personal morality is from his book, *The Hole in Our Gospel*. The hole is the failure of many evangelicals to give the attention and emphasis to caring for the needy that their faith demands. Pope Francis, in his apostolic exhortation *The Joy of the Gospel*, calls all Christians to a renewed emphasis on "works of love directed to one's neighbor [which] are the most perfect external manifestation of the interior grace of the Spirit."[7] The fact that Christians themselves have sometimes failed to fully live up to the tenets of their faith may have contributed to the belief that Christianity has only to do with worship and its rituals and celebrations. But it does not change the religious nature of such acts for the faithful who are responding to what their faith in fact demands of them.

Thread Number Two: Nondiscrimination Standards Unthinkingly Applied to Faith-Based Organizations

What should be done when nondiscrimination laws clash with faith-based organizations' religious beliefs? Almost all persons acknowledge that nondiscrimination laws have achieved much good. Women and racial minorities have job opportunities that were denied to them previously. One's religious background, as a general rule, may not be a basis for denying someone a job. Those with disabilities have opportunities for education and jobs they did not have previously. LGBT persons increasingly have more opportunities available to them. The United States is a more just, more equal society today because of nondiscrimination laws.

But there are times—not many, but there are times—when these nondiscrimination laws raise serious religious freedom questions. Potentially, they can clash with religiously based beliefs and practices.

Sometimes we as a society have handled potential clashes in a manner that safeguards both the nondiscrimination standards and organizations' religious freedom. For example, Title VII of the landmark 1964 Civil Rights Act outlawed employment discrimination on the basis of race, color, religion, sex, or national origin. But it also recognized that religious organizations—in order to maintain their religious character—should be able to make employment decisions based on religion. It therefore provided an exemption for religious organizations. It stated that the section of the law banning religious discrimination in hiring "shall not apply to . . . a religious corporation, association, educational institution, or society with respect to the employment of individuals of a particular religion to perform work connected with the carrying on by such corporation, association, educational institution, or society of its activities."[8] In short, the section forbidding religious discrimination in hiring does not apply to religiously based organizations. And the law made clear this was not limited to religious congregations. This section was upheld by a unanimous Supreme Court in 1987 in a case dealing with a faith-based gymnasium.[9] The ability of religiously based organizations to hire only persons in agreement with their religious missions was thereby protected; the right of persons to be hired regardless of their religion in all other circumstances was also protected. We have lived with this religious freedom protection for religious employers for fifty years with few questions or objections being raised.

Religious freedom problems can and have arisen, however, in other nondiscrimination areas. These have usually occurred when people were skeptical that faith-based schools, health service organizations, and social service agencies are fully religious. Recall the World Vision case where the employees who were let go insisted World Vision—because it did not look or act as a church—was not a religious but a humanitarian organization. As a result, nondiscrimination standards are at times arbitrarily applied to faith-based organizations without taking into account

"As applied to the nonprofit activities of religious employers, [the religious employment exemption in the Civil Rights Act] is rationally related to the legitimate purpose of alleviating significant governmental interference with the ability of religious organizations to define and carry out their religious missions."[10] —Justice Byron White, from the Supreme Court's opinion in *Corporation of Presiding Bishop v. Amos*

their religiously based beliefs. The religious freedom rights faith-based organizations assert are then viewed as claims to the right to inappropriately discriminate.

In addition, when faith-based and secular organizations provide similar services, many assume that those services must be exclusively secular in nature, even when provided by a faith-based organization. This is a false assumption. Those making this assumption fail to recognize that providing services to those in need is a *religious* act for the religious persons and organizations providing those services.

A 2002 study commissioned by the American Civil Liberties Union is revealing. It stated,

> Churches, temples, mosques, seminaries, and other pervasively sectarian institutions engaged in religious practices ought generally to be free of the requirements of laws repugnant to their beliefs. . . . When, however, religiously affiliated organizations move into secular pursuits—such as providing medical care or social services to the public or running a business—they should no longer be insulated from secular laws. In the public world, they should play by public rules.[11]

This outlook supports the right of religious congregations to follow the requirements of their faith traditions, even when they might run afoul of nondiscrimination laws. No one is arguing that a Catholic church should be forced to hire a woman as a priest, an evangelical church to marry a same-sex couple, or a synagogue to have a Christian as its rabbi. But the statement views those protections falling away when religiously based organizations move into what it terms "secular pursuits." In this mind-set they are now not engaged in religious acts but are providing secular services in the public world, and they must obey the public rules of the game, including nondiscrimination rules. But neither the ACLU nor anyone else has the right to define for the faithful what are and are not religious acts—and certainly not over the clear declarations of popes, pastors, and the voices of the faithful themselves. The assumption that the actions of faith-based organizations outside of prayer and religious ceremonies are thoroughly secular in nature is also illustrated by a document put out by the think tank we referenced earlier, Political Research Associates. At one point it refers to a judicial decision that "prioritized a secular American value (desegregation) over self-described religious values."[12] However, the attempt to distinguish a "secular American value (desegregation)" from "religious values" is misguided. The Reverend Martin Luther King Jr., if he were still living, would have problems calling desegregation a "secular value," as would hosts of brave demonstrators who marched out of their churches and into the streets in the 1960s. No one can thoughtfully read King's "I Have a Dream" speech and still claim desegregation and racial equality are simply secular values and contrast them with religious values.

> I have a dream that one day every valley shall be exalted, every hill and mountain shall be made low. The rough places will be made plain, and the crooked places will be made straight. And the glory of the Lord shall be revealed, and all flesh shall see it together [quoting Isaiah 40:4–5]. This is our hope. This is the faith that I go back to the South with. . . . With this faith we will be able to work together, to pray together, to struggle together.[13]

Limiting religion to what takes place within the four walls of "churches, temples, mosques, seminaries," to quote from the ACLU study, and labeling what to the faithful are deeply religious acts as "secular" is to misrepresent and distort religion. When this is done—as too often happens—nondiscrimination requirements can be applied to religious organizations in a way that violates their religious beliefs and standards.

The evangelical sorority and fraternity that were denied official recognition at San Diego State University were victims of the indiscriminate application of nondiscrimination standards. Their entrance into the public world of a state university required them to obey public nondiscrimination rules or leave the campus, even when those rules undermined the very nature of the organizations. Nondiscrimination on a religious basis should normally be a basic civil right and enforced on college campuses. We do not believe a vegan organization should be able to exclude all Catholics or all Jews. A student newspaper should not be able to exclude all Muslims from its editorial staff.

But in the case of *religiously based* student organizations, this nondiscrimination standard clashed with the students' right to form groups around their shared beliefs just as other students form groups around their shared beliefs. It is no more "discrimination" to say a religious group may have religious requirements for its members or leaders than for a sorority or fraternity to have gender requirements for its members, a Republican group to have political requirements for its members or leaders, or a LGBT student group to have requirements for its members or leaders based on attitudes toward sexual orientation. In all these examples, the membership standards of the student groups are not rooted in prejudice but in the very nature and purpose of the groups. The point of the organizations is to gather like-minded students together for mutual support and joint activities. Thus they do not constitute "discrimination" as we usually think of it.

The Catholic and evangelical adoption and foster care agencies in Illinois that faced state pressures to place children with same-sex and unmarried heterosexual couples is another instance of where a nondiscrimination regulation trumped the freedom of the faith-based agencies to act in keeping with their faith. The ability of same-sex and unmarried heterosexual couples to adopt children and provide foster care to abused or neglected children from all agencies clashed with the religious freedom of certain faith-based agencies. The nondiscrimination claims of the same-sex and heterosexual couples prevailed over the agencies religious freedom claims. Yet this was an unnecessary clash, since there were other agencies willing to service the unmarried couples. The issue was not one of whether or not unmarried couples would be able to adopt or provide foster care. No one was being denied the right to adopt children or provide foster care.

The reason the Illinois authorities ruled against the faith-based agencies is that they judged them to be violating nondiscrimination standards. Since the decision of the Illinois Circuit Court judge ruling against the faith-based agencies did not discuss their religious freedom claims, one cannot be certain why he felt those claims were not controlling in this situation. The assumption of the judge—as well as that of the Illinois Department of Children and Family Services and the Illinois legislature that has failed to pass legislation that would clarify the faith-based agencies religious freedom rights—seemed to be that by entering the worlds of state government contracts and adoption and foster care, the faith-based organizations had left the world of religious congregations and religious acts. Thus their religious freedoms were no longer protected. Nondiscrimination provisions applied to them as they would any secular child care agency. What is often called our first freedom, the freedom of religion, had to yield.

As more states and perhaps Supreme Court rulings move to allow same sex marriages, discrimination charges such as that faced by the Illinois Catholic and evangelical family service agencies are bound to increase. Marriage is an institution governed by civil law, but in most religious traditions it is also a religiously based institution. Some religious traditions will continue to hold that same sex marriages are not true marriages in their eyes even when they are recognized as legal marriages under civil law. Meanwhile, others—as the title of a *New York Times* editorial put it—will see "Religion as a Cover for Bigotry."[14] But to apply nondiscrimination standards to all faith-based organizations whose religious traditions view marriage as a bond only between one man and one woman is another instance of an inappropriate application of those standards. We as a society may disagree on the nature and limits of marriage, but to label organizations whose views of marriage are rooted in millennial-long, religiously based understandings of marriage as engaging in bigotry and discrimination is unwarranted.

As seen earlier, in the case of Title VII of the 1964 Civil Rights Act and its nondiscrimination hiring standards, our nation found a better way by providing an exemption for faith-based organizations. In most situations, desirable nondiscrimination regulations can coexist with religious freedom protections by providing reasonable exemptions for faith-based organizations with sincere, religiously rooted objections to certain nondiscrimination regulations. But for this to occur, at a minimum, we as a society must recognize these faith-based organizations are truly and fully religious organizations, and their acts are religious acts.

Thread Number Three: The Belief That Faith-Based Organizations That Accept Government Funds Become Government Actors

A third thread that ties together many of the religious freedom violations we discussed earlier is an assumption that once a faith-based organization accepts government funding for some of its programs—whether that funding is full or partial—it becomes an extension of the government; it becomes a state actor, an arm of the government. Thus, its actions become government actions. Since

"It is not the case that the religion-inspired policies and practices of institutions that receive public funds somehow become, for constitutional purposes, the government's own policies."[15] —Richard Garnett, professor, Notre Dame School of Law

government may not hold to certain religiously based standards in its actions, some conclude that a faith-based organization that has accepted government funds may not hold to those standards either. This belief can be seen in a number of the case studies we recounted in chapters 2 and 3. When it intervened in the court case over Catholic Charities adoption and foster care policies in Illinois, the state ACLU claimed, "Catholic Charities' in performing the exclusive government functions of placing adjudicated abused and neglected children who have been removed from their homes, are state actors. . . . As state actors, Catholic Charities may not assert religious defenses under state law because the State could not assert those defenses."[16] Because the State of Illinois largely financed the child care services the Catholic Charities agencies were providing they, in the opinion of the ACLU, had been transformed for all intents and purposes into government agencies—into extensions or branches of the government—and were subject to the same limits on their religiously based standards as would a government agency.

Similar reasoning can be found in the case concerning HHS's decision not to renew a grant to the United States Conference of Catholic Bishops (USCCB) for it to subcontract with agencies to provide help and support for victims of human trafficking. In fact, a Federal District Court ruled it would be unconstitutional for HHS to make any more grants to the USCCB victim support program. Key to the HHS and court decisions against funding the USCCB program is this third perspective or thread: the belief that a recipient of a government grant or contract becomes an extension or arm of the government and its actions become government actions. As seen in chapter 3, the District Court judge in the case brought by the Massachusetts ACLU reasoned that by awarding earlier grants to the USCCB—due to its faith-inspired position of requiring its subcontractors not to provide abortion or contraceptive services—the government had delegated to the USCCB the authority "to exclude certain services from government funding."[17]

This, in turn, provided the USCCB with "a significant symbolic benefit to religion, in violation of the Establishment Clause."[18]

It is wrong, however, to assume that a faith-based organization that receives government funding is thereby transformed into a branch or extension of the government and loses its religious freedom protections. One needs to ask, "Exactly what is going on when the government makes a grant to a faith-based nonprofit organization—or to a secular nonprofit organization for that matter?" Is it hiring that organization to act as its agent or proxy? Or is it an instance of the government and the nonprofit organizations seeing the same needs and seeking to work together to meet those needs? We believe it is the latter. The government—recognizing it does not possess all wisdom, all answers, and all on-the-ground resources to meet certain needs—turns to the huge world of nonprofit organizations to assist in meeting those needs by offering to partner with them by way of financial grants.

Appropriately, the term "independent sector" is often used to refer to this world of nonprofit health, educational, artistic, philanthropic, and social service organizations.[19] The Washington, DC–based organization Independent Sector describes its mission as advancing "the common good by leading, strengthening, and mobilizing the nonprofit and philanthropic community." Among its values is "a commitment to promoting and protecting the independence of the sector."[20]

Government grants and contracts to nonprofit organizations—whether faith-based or secular—create partnerships: government and nonprofit organizations working together to meet certain needs. But this does not transform the nonprofit organizations into government actors. Both the government agency making the grant or issuing the contract and the nonprofit organization receiving the grant or contract retain their identity and a clear measure of independence. One party in a partnership ought never to completely absorb or dominate the other party. Then it no longer is a partnership but the absorption of one entity into another.

President Obama's office dedicated to working with faith-based and nonprofit community organizations is the "White House Office of Faith-Based and Neighborhood Partnerships." The fact that the word "partnership" was purposely chosen is made clear by its website, which declares, "The White House Office of Faith-Based and Neighborhood Partnerships within the Domestic Policy Council works to form partnerships between the Federal Government and faith-based and neighborhood organizations to more effectively serve Americans in need."[21] "Partnership" refers to two distinct parties coming together to cooperate and work on a joint enterprise. Both parties in a partnership retain their identity and a certain measure of independence.

Government grants to nonprofit organizations function similarly, for example, to a private philanthropic foundation that, wishing to advance the role of the arts in a community, invites grant proposals from that community's arts organizations and then selects what it judges to be the most meritorious. No one would claim the recipient organizations thereby become arms or extensions of the foundation; it would be a foolish foundation that would attempt to dictate the actions of the recipient arts organizations. If the arts organizations are to remain independent, creative organizations, they need to maintain their own identity.

In the same way, faith-based and secular organizations that receive grants from the government or contract with the government to deliver certain services ought not to be swallowed up by government, thereby becoming its arms or extensions. The actions of "independent sector" organizations do not become government actions simply because government is helping to fund them.

In making grants or entering into certain contracts, the government may, of course, impose certain conditions and requirements. We are not saying the government must, so to speak, put a barrel of cash outside its doors and invite organizations—whether faith-based or secular—to come and help themselves, no questions asked. We are only saying that nonprofit organizations, including faith-based ones, should be able to compete for government-offered grants and contracts on the basis of the effectiveness and quality of their services without surrendering their identity and their distinctive contributions to the public good.

To say that a faith-based organization must jettison its religiously based hiring practices or certain religiously based standards to which its faith tradition holds—even though they do not affect the effectiveness of the services they would provide—in order to obtain a contract or grant is discriminatory. This was the case with the USCCB and HHS's awarding of the grants to other entities even though their own staff had ranked the USCCB's proposal as superior. And the United States District Court decision denied them the right to receive a grant, even if HHS had decided to award it to them, all because of the Catholic position on birth control and abortion. If USCCB overall—in light of all the other services it would have made possible—had the superior proposal, it should not be denied the grant. The USCCB and the organizations with whom it would subcontract should not be seen as agents or extensions of the government. They do not become government actors, and their policies do not become government policies. Instead, they are independent actors with resources, traditions, and a culture—and faith-inspired practices—independent of the government. The frequent failure to recognize this basic perspective contributes to the religious freedom problems of faith-based organizations we observed in the prior chapters.

Thread Number Four: The Belief That Christianity Is in a Dominant, Favored Position in Society

This brings us to the fourth and last thread that runs through the various instances of religious freedom violations we recounted in earlier chapters.[22] It is the belief that religion, and Christianity in particular, is in a dominant, privileged position in American society and politics. This belief can be seen in a reference a University of North Carolina history professor made to "Christianity's preferential place in our culture and civil law."[23] The study by Political Research Associates to which we made several references earlier makes passing reference to "Christianity's dominant position in American culture" and to "hegemonic Christianity."[24] Under this thinking, American culture and laws are infused with Christian references, and Christian advantages are enshrined in our laws and public policies.

None of the instances of religious freedom violations we have recounted explicitly turned on arguments that Christianity is in a dominant, privileged position. However, our years of experience in working with faith-based organizations and studying religious freedom issues have led us to the conclusion that many of the efforts to constrict or limit faith-based organizations' religiously based beliefs and practices are fed by the assumption that Christianity is in a privileged position in society. Attempts by Christian faith-based organizations to protect their religious freedom are then seen as attempts to use public policies to maintain or regain a favored position in society. When one makes this assumption, it follows that minority faiths and nonbelievers must be protected from a dominant Christianity that is seeking a privileged position for itself, often at the expense of others.

Superficially, this assumption may seem accurate. Our national motto is "In God We Trust," and it is assumed this is a Christian God, not the God or gods of Islam, Hinduism, or Buddhism. Throughout most of our history, there have been, and in a few places there still are, laws that restrict business activities on Sunday—the Christian holy day—and not on the Jewish Sabbath nor during Friday noon prayers observed by Muslims. Christmas is a national holiday; neither Yom Kippur nor *Eid al-Fitr*—marking the end of Ramadan—are. Every December the president lights the national Christmas tree. Each spring, stores are filled with Easter displays. Based on considerations such as these, many fear that if faith-based organizations' religious beliefs and practices are fully protected, Christianity, based on its numbers and long history of cultural influence, will exert inordinate influence and repress contrary faiths and beliefs.

This attitude helps to explain why Christian organizations are often slighted by the very persons who value "diversity." Go to the website of almost any college or university and one finds public commitments to diversity. The State University of New York at Buffalo has an Intercultural and Diversity Center that proclaims on its website, "The Center offers students various opportunities to engage in dialogue, celebrate differences and commonalities, and promote awareness about diversity and how it affects their beliefs, perceptions, and the global society."[25] San Diego State University has a separate tab labeled "Diversity starts here."[26] On its website, Vanderbilt University's Dean of Students states, "The Office of the Dean of Students creates opportunities to involve students, faculty, and staff in diverse learning communities."[27]

This is good and valuable. But many universities have a blind spot concerning how they put this commitment to diversity into practice. It is instructive to note that in all three of the universities cited here, Christian student organizations have struggled to keep from being denied official recognition and its accompanying campus privileges that other student organizations enjoy.

Why is this? How can a university proclaim its commitment to diversity on the one hand and deny official recognition to Christian student organizations on the other hand? Why is it committed to a pluralism that excludes Christian student organizations with distinctive beliefs and behavior standards? We believe the answer lies in the fact that many colleges' and universities' praise of and commitment to "diversity" is set in a context where Christianity is assumed to be in a privileged position. Diversity is rarely specifically defined, but from the examples given, universities seem to have in mind groups that have traditionally been minority groups in society and often the objects of discrimination and disrespect, such as women, racial and ethnic minorities, students from low income backgrounds, and LGBT students. Meanwhile, Christianity is assumed to be the privileged, dominant faith against which diverse minorities need to be protected and to find an identity.

But this thinking, if it was ever valid, is seventy or eighty years behind the times. We need to look beneath surface appearances. Christianity, in the sense of a faith that holds to the basic teachings of historic Christianity, is anything but culturally dominant in the United States today.

If Christianity is favored at all, it is a broad, generic Christianity. The God of "In God We Trust" is not the Triune God of historic Christianity. Christmas as a public holiday is more of a commercialized winter festival, and Easter a spring festival, than Christian observances of the birth or resurrection of Jesus Christ. Presidents and other public figures make references to God and his favor or presence, but these usually are references to a generic God invoked on ceremonial occasions or during times of national crisis or mourning. Supreme Court Justice William Brennan once wrote, "I would suggest that such practices as the designation of 'In God We Trust' as our national motto, or the references to God contained in the Pledge of Allegiance to the flag can best be understood . . . as a form a 'ceremonial deism,' protected from Establishment Clause scrutiny chiefly because they have lost through rote repetition any significant religious content."[28] This is a harsh but far from inaccurate description of the religious references found in our public life.

Surely such references to God or divine providence are far removed from the beliefs of the two major Christian traditions that hold most firmly to historic Christian teachings: evangelical Protestantism and Roman Catholicism. These traditions believe in a Triune God, the virgin birth of Jesus Christ, the reality of a life after death, the existence of a literal heaven and hell, and commands to conform one's life to certain divinely given standards.

Generalized public references to God or religion are far removed from the specific beliefs of these two major traditions. They are also far distant from Orthodox Judaism, which holds to beliefs and standards of behavior rooted in a millennia-old tradition and around which every Orthodox Jew is required to orient his or her life. The same can be said of practicing Muslims, Sikhs, and other religious adherents.

Evangelicals, Catholics, and Orthodox Jews are in anything but a privileged position in American society or law. Their political and cultural influence in society is severely limited. An evangelical pastor was removed from giving the closing prayer at President Obama's second inauguration because of his sincerely held beliefs on same-sex relationships. The centuries-old Catholic position on the immorality of abortion is often portrayed as a retrograde position and identified as part of a war on women. The evangelical and Catholic position on homosexual behavior has been described by a *New York Times* columnist as "a last bastion and engine of bigotry."[29] As we saw earlier in chapter 2, evangelicals elicited negative feelings on the part of a majority of university faculty members. A 2013 survey by the Tanenbaum Center for Interreligious Understanding found forty percent of white evangelicals reported they had experienced "a lot" of discrimination at work.[30]

As a result, there is a paradox present in American society today: traditional Catholics and evangelicals often feel marginalized, and their health, educational, and social service organizations are disadvantaged in the public realm; nonbelievers and nominal religious believers feel *they* are the ones being marginalized and subjected to unwanted religious pressures. We are convinced this basic fact underlies many of the religious freedom conflicts we cite in this book and makes resolving them more difficult.

We cannot state strongly enough that this book is *not* a plea for retaining or reinstating supposed advantages of Christian faith-based organizations. This book is a plea for a pluralism that accepts and tolerates the beliefs and practices of all faith-based

organizations—including those of Catholicism, evangelical Protestantism, and Orthodox Judaism—as well as the beliefs and
practices of other faiths' organizations and of secular organizations whose beliefs may run counter to traditional Christianity.
We believe in freedom of belief—or unbelief—for all, as well as
the freedom for all to live out their beliefs in the organizations
they have formed.

At the close of this chapter, we come back to the basic question: Why are there the violations of the religious freedom of
religiously based organizations in the United States today such
as those our earlier case studies chronicled? As we maintain and
explain in this chapter, we believe the root cause lies in the four
threads that weave the apparently disparate instances of religious
freedom violations together. These threads make up a set of beliefs
and assumptions—a mind-set or point of view. And once one accepts—implicitly or explicitly—this outlook and the threads that
make it up, what in fact are violations of religious freedom are
not seen as such. Given the outlook with which many begin, the
violations of organizational religious freedom we have observed
in this book are the natural, predictable end result. What is needed
is a new way of viewing and thinking about religious freedom as
it applies to religiously based organizations active in the public
realm. In the next chapter we develop this new way.

6

Free to Serve

Living with Our Differences

★

Many today are convinced a culture war is raging in the United States. In their view, religious persons and organizations in our society—usually Christian—are in a bitter struggle with non-religious, secular persons and organizations. One side opposes same-sex marriage; the other side favors it. One side supports prayers before legislative sessions; the other side opposes them. One side is "pro life" on abortion; the other side is "pro choice." And on and on.

It appears two irreconcilable visions are clashing. One vision holds that the United States was founded as a Christian nation and that its people are still predominantly Christian in character. Thus it is appropriate that Christian symbols and values infuse its public life. The other vision is that of a thoroughly secularized public realm, with all things religious banished to the private realm. Each side believes any loss in the public arena means their freedoms are violated.

At first blush it seems impossible to reconcile these positions. It appears to be a zero-sum game. One side's victory is the other side's defeat, and in time one side or the other will prevail. Fundraising letters and emails from groups on both sides add to this impression in their attempts to inspire persons to send them money. This culture war has spilled over into the issues of religious freedom for faith-based organizations. Those holding to a vision of a thoroughly secularized public realm believe Christian faith-based organizations—and those of other faiths—should be required to leave their faith behind when they enter the public realm. Especially when they accept government funding, they need to adhere to purely secular standards and practices. They have entered the public realm, and the public realm is a secular realm. Meanwhile, faith-based organizations believe they have every right to reflect their faith in their policies and practices. Otherwise, their freedom to serve in keeping with their religious faith is being violated. They would be squeezed into a secular mold destructive of their distinctive religious natures that lie at the heart of who they are.

However, this does not need to be a zero-sum game; one side's gain does not need to be the other side's loss. Much of the culture war rhetoric—and even the term itself—is rooted in the false assumption that one or the other of two opposing visions of our society and the public realm must prevail. Especially in the case of faith-based schools, health care programs, social service agencies, and many for-profit businesses, there is a third option.

"Mutual understanding is not the same thing as mutual agreement. . . . Only on a foundation of understanding can we seek a way to move forward, learning to live peacefully and respectfully with our differences."[1] —Jennifer Bryson, Director of the Islam and Civil Society Project, Witherspoon Institute

As we wrote at the outset in chapter 1, our pluralist vision of society equally respects and welcomes into the public life of the nation the wide diversity of religious and nonreligious beliefs, perspectives, and organizations. Both faith-based organizations and secular organizations have every right to enter the public realm, and—more important—they have a right to do so *as religious or secular entities*. Faith-based organizations should be free to serve as religious organizations true to their faith's tradition and not be squeezed into a secular mold, just as secular organizations should not be required to engage in religious activities, even of a very broad, generic nature. As intimated at various points in this book, this is what we favor. It is time to look more closely at this third option, one we have termed "principled pluralism."

Principled Pluralism: Its Basic Tenets

Principled pluralism rejects both a secularized public square and a religious—or a Christianized—public square in favor of a pluralist public square. Our vision is of an America in which we live together in tolerance and mutual respect notwithstanding our differences of race, color, ethnicity, national origin, gender, sexual orientation, *and religion*. This vision means our public policies must reflect and accommodate this tolerance and mutual respect.

Principled pluralism thereby rejects both government-enforced secularism and any kind of theocracy (government enforced adherence to a religion). Principled pluralism accepts the reality that our society is filled with diverse and sometimes clashing belief systems, both religious and secular in nature. We as a people follow different faiths; our consciences are formed in different ways. Diversity, to a greater or lesser degree, has always characterized the United States, and our system of religious freedom has always been a prime principle enabling us to live together with our deepest differences. Principled pluralism renews and clarifies this fundamental principle of American respect and tolerance.

Principled pluralism—or "civic pluralism" as it is sometimes called—is a political principle, a design for how a diverse people can live together in one political system. It requires neither that we agree completely with each other about our deepest beliefs (we don't) nor that we stop trying to convince each other about what we think is best (we shouldn't). Instead, principled pluralism simply asks us to agree to respect each other's convictions not only in private life but also in public life. Just as we ask for freedom to live our lives according to our convictions, we believe others with different convictions should be free to live their lives according to their convictions.

This means the public realm, our common life, will be neither Christian nor secular. The public realm ought not to privilege those of us who hold to Christian beliefs (or those of other religious traditions). Nor should secularism be imposed on all by banishing religion to the private world of congregational worship and personal devotions. Doing so would show little respect for people of faith—people for whom faith is relevant not only for worship but also for how they educate their children, heal the sick, serve the needy, and run a business. People of faith would then not be treated in a neutral, evenhanded manner. But the answer to such favoring of secularism cannot be to favor those with religious convictions and their organizations. That too is wrong.

Central to our position is the basic fact that a thoroughly secular world does not occupy neutral ground between belief and nonbelief. Instead, a nonreligious, secular perspective is a distinct perspective, or worldview, that is in competition with religious perspectives. Political scientist A. James Reichley was exactly correct when he once wrote, "Banishment of religion does not represent neutrality between religion and secularism; conduct of public institutions without any acknowledgment of religion *is* secularism."[2] This means a thoroughly secularized public realm has taken sides in the contest between religious and nonreligious organizations and their differing views of life and the world.[3] This is why principled pluralism not only seeks public policies that are evenhanded among the faith-based organizations of various religious traditions but also between faith-based organizations and secular organizations. Neither should be favored over the other.

We have referred to our position as being *principled* pluralism because there are indeed certain basic, underlying principles or tenets relating to human beings, society, and democratic freedom that are at its core. Four are particularly important.

Principled pluralism's first underlying tenet is that *all human beings are morally responsible, free individuals who possess human dignity and certain fundamental rights, the most basic of which is freedom of religion.* We selected our words carefully here. Freedom of religion has been referred to as our "first freedom" for more reasons than its appearing first in the Bill of Rights. The freedom of religious belief and practice is fundamental because it involves the deepest of human beliefs and practices—those that define who we are as persons. Freedom of religious belief and practice includes both what is often referred to as freedom of conscience and the free exercise of one's religious beliefs.

This hardly sounds revolutionary to American ears, yet it is fundamental to the other three tenets of principled pluralism. In the Judeo-Christian tradition—which is a deep source of our American values—the basis for human rights is the creation of all men and women by God in his image. This means they possess an inherent, God-given human dignity. This idea is made explicit in the Declaration of Independence's famous words, "All men [and women] are created equal and endowed by their Creator with certain unalienable rights." James Madison, in his famous "Memorial and Remonstrance," insisted that among these unalienable rights is freedom of religion.

We hold it for a fundamental and undeniable truth, "that religion or the duty which we owe to our Creator and the manner of discharging it, can be directed only by reason and conviction, not by force or violence." The Religion then of every man must be left to the conviction and conscience of every man; and it is the right of every man to exercise it as these may dictate. This right is in its nature an unalienable right.[4]

But principled pluralism does not stop here. There is more. Its second tenet is that *although human beings are individuals, with individual rights and responsibilities, human beings are also social beings*. We are made to live together in communities, not to live as separate, isolated individuals. The secluded hermit living off in a wilderness area by himself is an aberration, not the norm. That is why all societies down through the ages have been marked by families, clans, tribes, neighborhoods, and other social organizations.

American society is, in fact, composed of a wide variety of organizations such as churches, synagogues, and mosques; for-profit businesses; and a wide range of nonprofit service organizations, clubs, and associations. Often we come together in organizations that reflect a particular way of accomplishing some action. One scholar has estimated there are some 1.6 million nonprofit organizations in the United States.[5] There are churches of an astounding variety of denominations; Conservative, Reform, and Orthodox synagogues; and mosques of varying natures. There also are drug-treatment agencies that follow differing drug treatment approaches,

"The more authentically American alternative does not require [cultural liberals] to abandon their policy goals. . . . Rather, it just requires a rediscovery of pluralism's virtues, and the benefits of allowing different understandings of social justice to be pursued simultaneously, rather than pitted against each other in a battle to the death."[6] —Ross Douthat, *New York Times* columnist

"To coerce people towards Christianity is just as unacceptable as it is to coerce them away from it. Neither lies within the State's proper remit."[7] —Nick Spencer, research director of British think tank Theos

universities guided by secular or religious frameworks, and for-profit businesses that only offer "fair trade" goods and give much of their profits to marriage equality groups or that instead close on Sundays and give much of the profits to community religious groups.

This leads to a third basic tenet of principled pluralism: *For a society to be truly free its government must not prevent its members from being able to create and sustain nongovernmental organizations that are based on and reflect their members' deeply held beliefs.* A free society is one where persons are able—without smothering governmental coercion or interference—to form organizations that are rooted in and able to act on their freely decided beliefs and goals. This includes all types of secular and religiously based organizations.

Normally, men and women form their religious beliefs and then live out those beliefs not as isolated individuals but as members of families, religious congregations, charitable organizations, and more. That is why throughout this book we have made the point that for there truly to be religious freedom, religiously based organizations must be free. It is within them that believers come to faith and follow the demands of their faith. It is within churches and other religious congregations that the faithful gather to engage in worship, prayer, and their faith's rituals and celebrations. This is generally recognized. What is often missed, however, is that for many believers, religion is not merely something that takes place in a house of worship for one or two hours a week; it affects all aspects of their lives. This often includes banding together with others with shared beliefs to live out their faith together as they provide educational, health, and social services. Or they may band together with fellow believers to form a for-profit entity where they can follow their faith as businesspersons together.

A fourth and final tenet of principled pluralism is that *just as government should not attempt to dominate or control society's organizations and their members, neither should one organization seek to dominate or control other organizations or individuals.* One religion or religiously based organization must not seek—by law or other means—to impose its beliefs and practices onto other religious or nonreligious organizations and individuals. It should seek to protect its own beliefs and practices, not seek to impose its beliefs and practices onto others. Thus, at various points in this book, we have taken pains to make clear that the religious freedom rights we advocate for faith-based organizations are not aimed at controlling what organizations or persons of other faiths, or of no faith, may do; they are aimed at allowing religiously based organizations and their members to freely pursue their own religious beliefs and practices. By the same token—and this is a crucial point—nonreligious associations or advocacy groups ought not to seek to impose their beliefs onto persons of faith and their organizations. Respect and tolerance for each other must go both ways.

Three Additional Observations

To complete our description of principled pluralism, we need to make three additional observations. First, principled pluralism

"A Christianity that seeks to unilaterally impose itself on the nation is unlikely [to] be fruitful, but it is similarly unrealistic and unproductive to force a secular morality on believers."[8] —Michael Wear, former Obama White House staffer and writer for *The Atlantic*

means that *as faith-based organizations exercise their beliefs and follow their religiously based practices, they will sometimes inconvenience or burden others.* That is inevitable as we—unbelievers and believers coming from many different traditions—live together in one society. That is the small but real price that we must pay for living in a free society where each person's freedoms are protected. The inconvenience or cost each of us sometimes experiences makes possible the diversity and freedom our society rightly values.

One respects faith-based organizations—including those with which one differs—by allowing them to be distinctive in their beliefs and practices. This means, for example, that some social service agencies will have religious standards for its social workers, some hospitals will not perform sterilizations, and some businesses' health insurance plans will not cover contraceptives. Only when distinctive, religiously based practices such as these are safeguarded is the freedom of religious belief and practice protected. And this freedom means potential employees can find workplaces that are truly compatible with their convictions, and clients and customers are able to find providers of goods and services that share their convictions.

Admittedly, protecting religiously based practices such as these may impose a cost on others in the form of inconvenience or even what could be termed a burden. A secular social worker may have to seek out a secular social service agency in tune with her beliefs instead of applying for a job at a religiously based agency. A same-sex couple may experience the inconvenience of bypassing a religious adoption agency and having to find another one willing to assist them. The same-sex couple may even find it offensive that the religious agency believes it right and best for children not to be placed with them but with a mother-father married family. A person seeking a sterilization procedure at a Catholic hospital or clinic may have to go elsewhere to obtain this procedure.

However, experiencing costs of additional time and inconvenience is vastly different from actually being prevented from accessing a service, and it is wrong, we are convinced, for government to ban faith-based practices in the name of lifting an inconvenience or burden from others. Some faith-based adoption agencies have a policy, based on their view of marriage and family, not to place children with same-sex couples, whether married or unmarried. But this does not mean those couples must live in accordance with such agencies' religious beliefs. Adoptions by same-sex couples are legal in most places, and many agencies are ready, even eager, to work with them to arrange adoptions. Also, it is incorrect and highly misleading to say a Catholic hospital that does not perform sterilization procedures is thereby imposing its religious beliefs onto others. No, it is reflecting and acting on its own religiously based set of convictions. Those desiring a sterilization will have to go elsewhere to obtain it, but they can do so. No one is preventing them from obtaining that procedure. A female employee at an organization whose health insurance does not provide contraceptives has other ways to access contraceptives. There may be some added cost or inconvenience for her, but contraceptives are legal and available.

These are all examples of inconveniences or burdens that faith-based organizations' religious beliefs and practices sometimes impose on others, including those not of their faith. But that is the natural, inevitable result of a diverse public realm. We must weigh inconveniences and costs such as those in these examples with the violations of religious freedom that would be entailed in forcing faith-based organizations to violate their religious beliefs. If we as a society truly believe in the importance of religious diversity, we must surely resist imposing uniform practices onto others in violation of their religious beliefs. We must be willing to allow for and respect the differing religiously based practices of our fellow citizens. Public policy should allow for diverse ways of serving a diverse public.

It is important to recognize an additional point: persons of faith are sometimes inconvenienced or burdened by policies of secular organizations. Inconveniences and burdens go both ways. An evangelical psychologist who believes same-sex relations are sinful may be denied employment at a secular counseling agency that believes there are no social or moral problems with same-sex relations. A deeply religious person may be denied a job at an organization promoting atheism, even in a non–policy making position. A Catholic woman experiencing a problem pregnancy may feel compelled to leave a health clinic that sees abortion as a legitimate response and seek out a different clinic more committed to the time and expense of dealing with her medical challenges without resorting to abortion. An Orthodox Jew may be inconvenienced by having to seek out a hospital that serves kosher meals. We could multiply the examples.

In a society marked by diverse religious and nonreligious beliefs and practices, both the religious and the nonreligious will sometimes have to exercise forbearance and toleration as they experience inconvenience and burdens due to their fellow citizens living as their beliefs require them to live. That, we believe, is a small price we have to pay for a diverse society where persons of widely different traditions and beliefs can live and prosper together in peace.

A second crucial observation concerns the specific issue of abortion. In an important way *abortion poses an exception to principled pluralism's commitment not to impose its beliefs and practices onto others.* For many believers and their faith-based organizations, it is not enough if they themselves are not required to provide or take part in providing abortions. Their faith compels them to work to prevent others from providing them. Therefore, some may conclude that when organizations or individuals work to outlaw abortions on religious grounds, they are violating principled pluralism's commitment to protect people's and organizations' own religious freedom and not to seek to force their beliefs onto others.

But abortion is unique and it is important to see why. Here faith-based organizations and their supporters have every right to go beyond refusing to provide abortions themselves and work to make abortion illegal. This is not the place to go into a full-blown discussion of the abortion controversy. Many others have done so elsewhere. From this book's religious freedom perspective, however, the crucial starting point is the basic, scientific fact that abortion ends a human life—in the early stages of pregnancy a small, nascent, not-fully-developed human life, but a human life nonetheless.

Many on the pro-choice side of this issue argue that a woman's right to control her reproductive life, as it is often put, takes precedence over the human life that abortion ends. But that does not negate the fact that in a vital manner the abortion decision is one that has direct, irreversible results for a human life other than that of the woman obtaining the abortion. Pro-choice advocates can argue that the mother's rights trump those of the unborn, but they cannot deny the fact of the unborn human life and thus that an abortion decision affects more than simply the pregnant woman.

This means that when religiously motivated persons and organizations seek to end legal access to abortions—even for persons who reject their beliefs and are not members of their organizations—principled pluralism is not violated. We as a society have long accepted that many religiously supported positions—such as those against stealing, driving while drunk, and lying under oath—can and should also be illegal under our civil laws. Why? Because they have consequences that harm others and society. As the old saying goes, "My freedom to swing my arm ends where your nose begins!" It was on this basis that the nineteenth-century abolitionists—many of whom were driven by their religious beliefs—worked to end slavery everywhere. It was not enough that they themselves not own slaves.

It is on this basis that we argue the issue of abortion is in a different, special position compared to the other religious freedom questions we consider in this book. When it comes to abortion, religiously motivated persons have a right to attempt, by peaceful, democratic means, to influence public policy and court decisions so as to limit its availability, just as others have the right to argue the contrary position.

A third observation is that *our position is* principled *pluralism, not what can be called fallback pluralism or expediency pluralism.* We do not advocate pluralism as a second-best, fallback position to which religious folks retreat when they are unable to maintain advantages or a privileged position for themselves in society and in public policy. Nor is it simply a pluralism created to meet an expedient desire to retain a place for faith in the public realm. We advocate something quite different. Given the diversity of beliefs and practices in today's world, we are committed to advancing religious freedom rights for persons of all faiths and of none as a principled commitment.

Are There Limits to Organizations' Religious Freedom?

All rights have certain limitations or bounds on them. The First Amendment right to freedom of speech, as Chief Justice Charles Evan Hughes once famously wrote, does not give one the right to falsely shout "Fire!" in a crowded theater and cause a panic. And our freedom of expression is limited by laws against libel and slander. So also the religious freedom for organizations we advocate here under principled pluralism has certain limits. Principled pluralism does not assert organizations' religious freedom rights always and necessarily trump all other rights or values. To complete our understanding of principled pluralism and how it should be applied to the organizational religious freedom issues our society is facing today, we need to point out certain limits on organizations' religious freedom—and on the diversity and pluralism we are advocating. Three are especially important.

A religiously based organization cannot claim religious freedom protection for acts of violence or for planning and urging the use of violence. Our society long ago decided that the freedom we all prize does not include the right to plan, plot, and advocate the use of force and violence to achieve its ends or to overthrow the government. Claiming a religiously rooted basis for violent acts is no more a protection for them than a secular claim would be.

A second limitation on organizations' robust religious freedom and the resulting pluralism we are advancing here is that it *does not include the activities and beliefs of religiously based organizations that are rooted in hatred, fear, blind prejudice, and a desire to repress others.* The Ku Klux Klan has, for example, claimed some sort of religious basis for its words and acts of hatred. It and other white supremacist organizations ought not to be able to claim religious freedom, and the diversity and pluralism it enables, as a protection for their hatred, prejudice, and attempts to repress others. They should be able to claim—and indeed have claimed— protection based on the freedom of expression and association. The courts will continue to evaluate the constitutionality of such claims. We are only saying here that the religious freedom rights and the resulting religious diversity we are advancing in this book are not additional bases for protecting an organization such as the Ku Klux Klan.

Underlying both of these first two limitations is the fact that we are a society, and to be a society, there must be forces that bind us together. A society and a political community is more than many individuals who happen to live in the same geographic area or a multitude of associations with no values or other beliefs in common. There must also be certain beliefs, traditions, and a commitment to the general welfare—to the common good or the public interest—that bind a people together, otherwise they are not a people. Principled pluralism is based on the rights of diverse organizations with diverse values and beliefs, but it is also based on mutual respect. One group must not seek to exclude another group from the public realm, claiming its right to exist and to follow its beliefs is illegitimate.

Our coins proclaim *E Pluribus Unum* ("Out of many one"). Both "*pluribus*" and "*unum*" must be given their due. We stress in this book "*pluribus*," since we believe in the case of faith-based organizations we as a society have been losing sight of our "many-ness" and the importance of protecting it. But the principled pluralism we advocate here does not urge that we lose sight of what also binds us into one nation. That is why religions and their organizations that teach and practice violence, hatred, fear, blind prejudice, and attempts to repress others cannot share in the religious pluralism and its attendant freedoms we advocate here.

A final limitation on what we are advancing in this book is a requirement that *an organizations' religiously based beliefs and practices that are to be protected must be well-grounded and sincerely held.* They cannot be idiosyncratic beliefs trumped up to serve some nonreligious cause. If we are to remain one society united by common traditions, beliefs, and policies, organizations' religious freedom rights must rest on sincerely held beliefs that are genuinely grounded in religious convictions. Respect for those who differ from us must be granted, but in a sense it must also be earned by way of thoughtful, sincere beliefs.

The sincerity of religious beliefs can easily be demonstrated when they are rooted in a known, long-standing religious tradition. It is hardly surprising when a Catholic Charities agency has objections to including contraceptives in its health care policy. Or when an evangelical adoption agency challenges a requirement they place children with a same-sex couple. Or when an Orthodox Jewish butcher has objections to slaughtering animals by means that violate ancient Jewish dietary laws. Religion, by its very nature, is a shared experience. It is almost always rooted in a tradition that is known, shared by many persons, and practiced within congregations and other associations.

Room should of course be made for faith-based organizations that are asserting certain religious freedom protections that are unique to them or based on newly identified concerns as social practices and government regulations change. Their religious free-dom should also be protected unless the claimed protections rest on beliefs whose sincerity are highly suspect.

Admittedly, there will be some close calls in terms of when any of these limitations should limit claimed religious freedom rights of faith-based organizations—or should not do so. We will deal with this question more fully in chapter 8, where we consider some questions that can be raised in connection with our vision of principled pluralism. There are legal standards—such as those in the Religious Freedom and Restoration Act (RFRA) we referred to in earlier chapters—that give a basis for the courts to make these close calls.

The point we wish to make here is that not one of the instances of religious freedom violations we cited earlier in this book run counter to any of these three limitations on religious freedom as protected by principled pluralism. They are not close calls. Most of the organizations that are running into religious freedom problems today are rooted in the Roman Catholic or evangelical Protestant traditions. These are major, long-standing traditions going back hundreds, even thousands, of years. They comprise about fifty percent of the American population.[9] And their beliefs—whether one accepts them as true or not—are based on concepts rooted in their holy Scriptures, in their understandings of natural law, and in their traditions' theological reflections. They long precede today's issues. They have not been newly minted to avoid compliance with policy positions now in ascendancy. The exact same point can be made in regard to religious freedom issues that have arisen in regard to Orthodox Jews, Muslims, Sikhs, Native Americans, and other religious minorities.

The four tenets of principled pluralism and the observations and limitations we have outlined in this chapter work together to achieve the goal we have put forward many times in this book: a pluralist public realm where persons of all religious faiths and of none are free not only to worship or refrain from worship as their beliefs dictate but also free to act as citizens and to follow their faith's demands in organizations they have formed. We seek no less and no more than this.

We as a nation are a people of diverse convictions. We worship differently or not at all; we develop and patronize different kinds of service organizations; we desire different kinds of employment environments. When organizations are diverse, none will be right for everyone. One size fits all is neither the reality nor the goal. But that's just the point. We are diverse, we value different things, we seek to serve in different ways. Principled pluralism allows us to deal with this reality of differences without resorting either to theocracy or enforced secularism.

Will Pluralism Survive the Death of Relativism?

KIM COLBY

Relativism is dead. But unlike 1966—when *Time* magazine ran its controversial cover asking "Is God Dead?"[1]—in 2014, little public notice has been given to relativism's passing. Nonetheless, if we are to understand the current threats to pluralism and religious liberty, we must realize that relativism is indeed dying or dead on most American university campuses and in the public square. Relativism's skepticism that truth exists and its encouragement of the "marketplace of ideas" are being replaced by an unyielding ideology, "Truth 2.0," which claims superiority to all competing ideas, including traditional Christianity.

1. See Phillip Goldberg, "Revisiting *Time*'s 'Is God Dead?' Cover," April 21, 2014, available at http://www.huffingtonpost.com/philip-goldberg/revisiting-times-is-god-d_b_5183667.html.

For the latter half of the twentieth century, Western Christians saw relativism as the primary ideological threat to Christianity and Jesus's central claim that "I am the way and the truth and the life" (John 14:6). Relativism's untenable belief that all ideas are equally true—or more likely, equally false—flourished after World War II as the West grappled with the most destructive war unleashed in human history and the staggering barbarism the war exposed in highly educated, highly cultured Europe. Relativism offered a shallow ideological refuge to a Western culture that was weary of ideological conflict and wary of claims of ideological truth.

But for all its flaws, relativism was at least philosophically friendly to pluralism and religious liberty. By definition, relativism necessarily accepted a diversity of worldviews, beliefs, and values. To avoid hypocrisy, relativism had to respect the right of individuals to hold differing versions of truth. In theory if not always in practice, relativism had to accept that any religious belief, including Christianity, might be true and was at least equally as valid as any other ideological belief. Such an approach was conducive to religious liberty.

Not so the philosophy that is rapidly displacing relativism. The new philosophy, which I term "Truth 2.0," holds that certain fundamental truths do exist but equally holds that traditional Christianity is decidedly not one of them. Indeed, a basic tenet of "Truth 2.0" is that traditional Christianity is not only false but also harmful, if not evil. At base, the disciples of "Truth 2.0" will not tolerate traditional Christianity because its beliefs transgress their most fundamental truth: an individual's sexual autonomy must be unhindered, even unquestioned, no matter what the cost to others' liberty or even to others' right to life. Its disciples demand that everyone must agree that abortion and sexual conduct outside of traditional marriage are not only acceptable but affirmatively good. Dissent from this embrace of absolute sexual autonomy will not be tolerated, even if that dissent is grounded in a deep belief that human beings bear God's image from conception throughout life.

While inherently compatible with a culture of relativism, pluralism can also coexist with a culture that holds to a specific truth. For two centuries in America, despite a rocky start and several detours, pluralism coexisted with Christianity's claim to truth.

Pluralism is inherently compatible with evangelical Christianity because it mirrors three core evangelical beliefs.[2] First, pluralism can be understood as an extension of the basic evangelical Christian precept of the "priesthood of all believers." That is, pluralism respects the individual's autonomy of conscience because pluralism accepts the possibility that individuals may perceive truth even when society's elites do not. Therefore, pluralism refuses to restrict the individual's exercise of conscience unless necessary to protect others from physical harm.

Second, pluralism derives from the Christian belief that God gave each human free will to choose whether to accept his truth. If God, who knows what truth is, gives human beings the choice to accept or not accept truth, then fallible human institutions, including government, ought to give individuals great deference in their choices as to what they accept as truth. As Isaiah 1:18 remarkably illustrates, God chooses reason rather than coercion in dealing with humans: "'Come now, and let us reason together,' says the LORD, 'though your sins are as scarlet, they will be as white as snow; though they are red like crimson, they will be like wool'" (NASB). If God is willing to reason with human beings, despite our sinfulness, then we Christians understand that we should make every effort to reason with rather than coerce our fellow humans.

Third and most important, pluralism is a straightforward application of the Golden Rule to our civic relationships: to do to others as we would have them do to us (Luke 6:31). Pluralism thrives only if citizens treat one another as they themselves wish to be treated. Each citizen with his or her individual ideas, values, and beliefs, is to be treated with respect, reason, and humility. Respect, because each of us is made in God's image and granted free will to choose whether to accept his truth or not. Reason, because God deigns to reason with us despite our wrongdoings. Humility, because we know that we are

2. James Madison evokes many precepts of the Christian faith in his explication of religious liberty, the *Memorial and Remonstrance against Religious Assessments* (1785), reprinted in *Everson v. Board of Education*, 330 U.S. 1, 63 (1947) (appendix).

fallible human beings falling short—far short—of the glory of God (Rom. 3:23).[3]

Pluralism can thrive in a culture informed by Christian truth. Pluralism likewise can thrive in a culture of relativism and skepticism. But whether "Truth 2.0" will tolerate pluralism is much less certain. The initial signs are ominous. As this book chronicles, "Truth 2.0" recently has shown itself to be openly hostile to both pluralism and religious liberty.[4] We hope, perhaps futilely, that pluralism can coexist in a culture in which sexual appetite defines the new truth. But perhaps a culture that rejects self-restraint is incapable of the respect, reason, and humility that pluralism demands. If so, we will lose the principled pluralism upon which our religious liberty depends.

....

Kim Colby is a graduate of Harvard Law School and director of the Christian Legal Society's Center for Law and Religious Freedom.

....

3. In his excellent article exploring similar themes, "A Confident Pluralism," John Inazu urges a "confident pluralism" built on "tolerance, humility, and patience." John D. Inazu, "A Confident Pluralism," 88 (forthcoming in *Southern California Law Review*, 2015) (draft available at http://papers.ssrn.com/sol3/papers.cfm?abstract_id=2470788).

4. See, e.g., remarks of Professor Katherine Franke, "Symposium on Religious Accommodation in an Age of Civil Rights," Harvard Law School, April 3–5, 2014, available at https://www.youtube.com/watch?v=IWwTXiqngzg (beginning at 44:45).

7

Free to Serve

Faith-Based Organizations in the Public Realm

★

What specific, concrete difference does our vision of organizations' religious freedom make as faith-based organizations seek to follow their faith's demands in the realm of public programs and services? We wrote this book to be something other than an academic exercise. Therefore, we need to apply the concept of principled pluralism, and the organizational and personal freedoms it protects, to the case studies of religious freedom abuses we presented earlier in chapters 2 through 5. As we do so, we will clarify the practical differences principled pluralism makes in the real world of faith-based organizations as they provide services to the public.

Staff, Leaders, and Members Selected by Conviction and Conduct

Chapter 2 related two case studies of faith-based organizations that faced challenges to their ability to determine who could or could not be a member, leader, or employee. One case study dealt with Christian student organizations being refused on-campus privileges because they had Christian belief or behavior standards for their members and leaders, and the other dealt with World Vision, an evangelical worldwide relief and development agency, and its right to let staff members go who no longer were in agreement with its clear, stated religious beliefs. Both of these cases are examples of what in chapter 5 we referred to as nondiscrimination standards being applied to faith-based organizations in an inappropriate manner.

Principled pluralism begins its approach to disputes such as these by distinguishing between arbitrary, invidious discrimination on the one hand, and rational discrimination on the other. The general rule is that individuals should not be denied employment or membership in organizations, nor experience other social limitations simply because of their race, ethnicity, gender, religion, or sexual orientation. To do so would be invidious discrimination. But we all also recognize that sometimes such distinctions are relevant to the very nature and purpose of a group. Arbitrary discrimination differs from making reasonable, even necessary distinctions. Thus a college sorority may rationally refuse to admit men, a Republican organization may refuse to hire a Democrat as its executive director, and an LGBT support group may refuse to hire someone who recently led a campaign against the legalization of same-sex marriage. Making distinctions such as these constitute rational, appropriate discrimination. It allows and protects a diversity of organizations representing a diversity of points of view. This is right and proper. The freedom to be whom we wish to be and to advocate for what we believe is protected.

Religiously based groups should be part of the diversity and pluralism of our society, and this extends beyond churches and other religious congregations to include the wide variety of educational, health, and social service organizations. Through such organizations, people of a like-minded religious faith can band together and, in obedience to their faith, develop programs and provide services for those in need.

Therefore, universities should be open to student organizations based on ethnic, sexual orientation, political, and other points of view or identifications, including religious points of view and identifications. Just as a Republican or Democratic student organization should be able to limit its membership or leaders to those in political agreement with the views around which it is organized, so also an evangelical, Catholic, Muslim, Jewish, Sikh, or other religious organization should be able to do so if it so desires. It is no more wrongful discrimination for a Jewish student organization to limit its membership or leaders to Jews than it is for an environmental student organization to limit its membership to students in agreement with its goal of greater protections of the natural environment. Both the Jewish and the environmental student organizations may decide to admit as members, and perhaps even as leaders, persons who are not Jews or environmentalists, but that should be their choice.

Institutional pluralism such as this protects the diversity of university campuses and promotes a lively exchange of ideas and views. The ideal of diversity on campuses is not simply a diversity of individuals living separately as individuals, nor is it a number of student organizations, each with a similar mix of persons, in terms of race, ethnicity, sexual orientation, political views, and religion. Instead, a truly diverse campus is one where a wide variety of student organizations are free to form around particular points of view or shared characteristics. Especially for persons from groups that may feel like outsiders on a large, secular university campus—such as racial and ethnic minorities; students from low-income backgrounds; LGBT students; and serious, practicing Catholics and evangelicals—it is important to be able to band together for mutual support and friendship and to work together to be heard in the exchange of ideas that marks healthy college and university campuses.

"Throughout American history, gays and lesbians, like other disfavored minorities, have struggled to speak collectively without fear of government sanction, and the formation of expressive associations has often represented the first step toward equality. Wooden and inflexible application of nondiscrimination provisions to expressive associations like [the Christian Legal Society student chapter] will erode the right to choose one's associates, thereby threatening the ability of disfavored minorities to associate to express their views free from majoritarian interference."[1] — From the *amicus* brief of Gays and Lesbians for Individual Liberty in *Christian Legal Society v. Martinez*

Tish Harrison Warren, whose essay appears earlier in this book, is an Anglican priest who works with InterVarsity Christian Fellowship, a network of evangelical student organizations. She accurately expressed the position to which principled pluralism holds in discussing a situation at Vanderbilt University.

> Because true diversity can be messy and contentious, the human tendency regarding pluralism is often to flatten differences and stamp out unpopular ideologies. Irreconcilable ideologies produce conflict; conflict threatens peace. However, the proper resolution is not to abrogate conflicting ideologies, but to learn to embody our robust particularities respectfully and intelligently. . . . This is the promise of pluralism—that communities can have opposing ideologies, yet not silence one another, but instead learn to live as neighbors and, more radically, as friends.[2]

We could not express it better.

Some universities have handled the issue of on-campus recognition of religiously based student organizations in an appropriate manner. In April 2013 the University of Michigan issued the following statement:

Free speech and diversity, including religious diversity, are core principles at U-M. We value the existence of the Asian InterVarsity Christian Fellowship, along with the other 69 faith-based student organizations at U-M. Their existence and their voices add significantly to our academic community and support those students who find solace, camaraderie and guidance in their presence.[3]

Similarly, Ohio State University has made the following provision: "A student organization formed to foster or affirm the sincerely held religious beliefs of its members may adopt eligibility criteria for its Student Officers that are consistent with those beliefs."[4] These are examples of principled pluralism in action.

The second case study we considered in chapter 2 concerned World Vision and its letting three staff members go because they no longer were in agreement with its religiously based mission. The fired employees claimed World Vision was merely a humanitarian, not a religious, organization and thus could not legally make employment decisions based on religion. Principled pluralism says the Court of Appeals got it right—even if by a narrow two-to-one margin—when it held World Vision is indeed a religiously based organization and thus had the right to make employment decisions based on religion. It was not an instance of arbitrary discrimination.

Principled pluralism protects religious freedom by insisting, first, that public-serving organizations such as World Vision can be truly and fully religious in nature. Second, as religious organizations, they may make employment decisions in keeping with their faith when they consider it important to do so to safeguard the religious nature of their organizations. As seen earlier in chapter 5, Title VII of the 1964 Civil Rights Act appropriately protects the right of religiously based organizations to make employment decisions based on religion. But this freedom would be of only limited value in protecting religious freedom if it applied only to religious congregations and not to schools, overseas development agencies, hospitals, and other faith-based organizations.

The error the three fired employees and the dissenting judge made in this case was to assume that only religious congregations can be truly and fully religious. Since World Vision did not look or act like a church, they claimed it could not be a religiously based organization whose religious freedom was protected. However, walling religion off from the public realm and relegating it to the private realm of religious congregations and their rituals and celebrations violates the very nature of religion—what it means to be religious and what religion requires of its followers. Instead, a proper understanding of religious freedom protects the religious identity of public-serving organizations of all religious faith.

Religious freedom is both an outgrowth of and a contributor to a diverse, pluralist public realm. It is an outgrowth of a pluralist public realm since a truly pluralist public realm frees faith-based organizations to maintain their religious character; it is a contributor to a pluralist public realm because they add to the diversity of the public realm. Principled pluralism thereby looks to a diversity of organizations as the surest safeguard of religious freedom for all. It does not seek to squeeze all faith-based organizations into a secular mold.

We also believe the freedom to make employment decisions based on the beliefs of prospective employees should be extended to organizations dedicated to promoting a secular system of belief. The Freedom from Religion Foundation, a nationwide organization, is such an organization. Its website states that it is "the nation's largest association of freethinkers (atheists, agnostics, and skeptics) with over 19,000 members."[5] It should be able to limit its paid staff to "atheists, agnostics, and skeptics" just as organizations such as World Vision, Catholic Relief Services, and Jewish Vocational Services should be able, if they so desire, to limit their paid staff to persons in religious agreement with them.

One related and important point: for religious freedom purposes, the freedom to make hiring decisions based on religious beliefs does not change when faith-based organizations receive some government funding for the services they provide to the public. When government sees a faith-based organization providing certain services it believes have important public benefits—such as health care in a low-income neighborhood, drug treatment for the addicted, or help to victims of human trafficking—it may decide that, for the public good, it wishes to enable that organization to continue or expand those services. Thus government may enter into a partnership with the faith-based organization. The government, with its taxing powers and greater financial resources, helps fund the services being provided, and the faith-based organization provides additional funding, dedicated staff, and outreach into the needy community.

As we highlighted in chapter 5, when the government helps fund the activities of a faith-based organization, it does not become an arm or extension of the government as some assume; the government does not swallow up its partner and turn it into a clone of government agencies. It does not become a government actor. Principled pluralism insists that faith-based organizations—and secular nonprofit organizations as well—should retain a significant measure of independence and freedom of action. And this includes the freedom to maintain their religious character by hiring staff who support their religiously based missions. Otherwise, the end result of government funding is a gray sameness, with faith-based organizations losing their distinctive religious character and becoming much like secular, nonprofit or government agencies. Often it is because of the religious commitment and practices of faith-based organizations that they are effective. Requiring them to give up their religious character would undermine the very reason that they were seen by government as desirable partners in meeting certain needs.

The threats to the ability of organizations receiving government funding to hire only persons who support their religious mission are real, yet three different presidential administrations of both political parties have protected this right. Happily, Presidents Bill Clinton, George W. Bush, and Barack Obama have all taken special care that federal funding rules enable faith-based organizations to enter into financial partnerships with government without abandoning their religious character. But the threat remains in the form of more than a few public officials, judges, media outlets, and advocacy groups.[6]

When Laws and Faith Collide

At times the government enacts laws and regulations that—although enacted for the good of society as a whole—clash with specific religious beliefs or practices of certain religious groups. This raises a question: if a public policy enacted to advance the public good has the side effect of encroaching on the religiously based practices of some faith-based organizations, must the public policy or the religiously based practices yield?

We have faced this situation before in our history. Military draft laws, enacted for the protection of the nation and perhaps for its very survival, clash with religious groups that hold to pacifism as a fundamental belief. Laws requiring parents to send their children to school through the age of sixteen have conflicted with some Amish groups that believe, on religious grounds, their children's education should end with the eighth grade. Abortion, through most stages of pregnancy, has been made a legally protected right by the Supreme Court, but many hospitals, doctors, and nurses have deeply felt religious objections to taking part in providing abortions. In these cases—and many others we could cite—should religious freedom be protected, or should the right of society to enforce public policies it has judged benefit the public good trump religious freedom?

The answer we as a society have often given is to exempt those with sincere, religiously based objections from legal requirements. We have provided exemptions from the military draft for religious pacifists. Often alternative forms of service were required, but even when the nation was under serious military threat, we have respected those with conscientious objection to participating in war. In a Supreme Court decision, the Amish were granted an exemption to the law requiring parents to send their children to school through age sixteen.[7] Soon after the Supreme Court's 1973 *Roe v. Wade* decision that held women had a constitutionally protected right to abortion, Congress passed what was called the Church Amendment (named after the then Democratic Senator from Idaho, Frank Church). It provides that no health professional or institution can be required to take part in an abortion or sterilization procedure "if his performance or assistance in the performance of such procedure or abortion would be contrary to his religious beliefs or moral convictions."[8] Granting exemptions to believers from otherwise valid laws when they clash with their beliefs is among the best of our traditions.

Additional protections for those with religious objections to certain legal requirements were gained in 1993 when a nearly unanimous Congress passed and President Bill Clinton signed the Religious Freedom Restoration Act (RFRA). This crucial law— which we considered earlier in chapter 4—appropriately created a balancing test that was weighted in favor of protecting religious freedom. Religious freedom claims to exemptions from valid public policies do not necessarily prevail, but the government has a high bar to clear if it is to restrict an individual's or an organization's religiously based practices. As seen in chapter 4, RFRA provides that public policies may not "substantially" burden the free exercise of religion, even in the case of a law aimed at promoting the public

"Religious exemptions date back to the Revolution and even the colonial era, because America has always been committed to certain kinds of multiculturalism."[9]—Eugene Volokh, professor, UCLA School of Law

good not at restricting religious freedom but that would inadvertently have that effect for some.[10] Thus, religious organizations cannot claim an exemption for every minor or inconsequential religious freedom violation. They must demonstrate the public policy imposes a "substantial" burden on their religious freedom. But the government must demonstrate—once it has been established there is a substantial burden on religious freedom—that the public policy is furthering "a compelling government interest" by the least restrictive means.

Because of a Supreme Court decision, RFRA applies only to the federal government, but twenty states have passed their own RFRA laws that are very similar to the federal one. By passing RFRA Congress acknowledged the importance of not requiring persons and organizations to violate their religious beliefs and gave additional protections when legal requirements would demand them to do so.

In summary, both by precedent and by law, we as a society have supported exemptions for religious organizations when there are public policies that would require them to act contrary to their significant religious beliefs, even when those policies are rooted in what the Supreme Court has held to be a constitutional right.

Principled pluralism and its understanding of religious freedom say that when a law or regulation collides with religiously based organizations' religious beliefs and standards—such as the ones we cite in chapters 3 through 5—the normal policy should be to grant those organizations and their members exemptions from the law or regulation. That is the preferred way to protect the religious freedom rights of all. That, as we have just seen, is the path we as a nation have usually taken.

Thus, when, as we saw in chapter 3, Arizona and Alabama enacted laws that forbade faith-based groups from providing transportation, food, shelter, and other care to the needy without first screening out undocumented immigrants, those laws were forbidding certain faith-based organizations to act as their faith demanded. Arizona and Alabama attempted to impose a uniformity of practice in the name of good public policy aimed at what they viewed as a serious problem. Since the faith-based organizations were operating in the public sphere, they would just have to conform. "Keep your faith-based practices within the four walls of your churches," seemed to be the attitude.

Principled pluralism insists that when believers move from the world of religious congregations, worship services, and private devotions into the world of providing educational, health, and other public services, they have not left a religious world for a secular world. If they are not free to follow their faith from Monday to Saturday as well as on Sunday, their religious freedom is being infringed upon. In this case, the state governments were wrong to forbid certain faith-based organizations to do what their religious beliefs required them to do. This affected both the organizations and their cultures, values, and purposes as faith-based organizations as well as the ability of individuals to practice their faith within those organizations.

Under our vision of pluralism, the states of Arizona and Alabama, if they were indeed convinced of the desirability of the laws they enacted, should have provided for an exemption from the requirements of the law to accommodate the beliefs of religious congregations and other faith-based organizations. The public realm should no more be a secularized realm where religious beliefs and standards have no applications or protections than it should be a religious realm where all are forced to act according to Christian or other religious norms.

Another case study of attempts to require faith-based organizations to act contrary to their religious beliefs concerned evangelical and Catholic family service agencies in Illinois. In that case the state pressured these agencies, on pain of losing grants they had been receiving for forty years, to place foster care and adoptive children with unmarried couples, both same sex and heterosexual. The evangelical agency and several Catholic Charities agencies

stopped doing foster care and adoption placements as part of a
state-funded program rather than violate their religious beliefs.
Pushing them to this decision was unnecessary and unwise. There
were other family service agencies willing to place children with
same-sex and other unmarried couples, and the faith-based agencies who in good conscience could not do so were willing to refer
unmarried couples to agencies which would do so. No one was
being denied the opportunity to adopt or provide foster care to
needy children.

This is an instance of nondiscrimination regulations being applied in an unthinking, arbitrary manner. Faith-based agencies
with sincere, religiously based objections to placing children with
same-sex or unmarried heterosexual couples should have been
granted an exemption by Illinois. Since there were other, well-
known agencies willing to place children with such couples, there
would have been no great public loss—even from the point of view
of Illinois—if a religious exemption had been allowed. Illinois in
effect said, "If you violate your religious beliefs by placing children
with unmarried couples, you can continue to receive the annual
contracts as you have for forty years; if you are unwilling to do so,
we will cut you off from further contracts." It would have been a
simple matter to allow an exemption for religiously based agencies
having religious scruples against placing children with same-sex
and unmarried couples. All family service agencies do not have
to be the same; all do not have to adhere to the same standards.
Some couples may prefer going to an agency that is in its own
faith tradition; others may prefer a secular agency. And that is
okay. This is what pluralism, diversity, and tolerance are about.

Instead, both the Illinois Department of Children and Family
Services and the court that ruled in the Department's favor got it
wrong. In the name of nondiscrimination, they promoted a uniform, secular public realm, not a diverse public realm. Pluralism
and diversity were lost as the range of faith-based organizations
providing certain services was narrowed and the public had fewer

"Furthermore, punishing Plaintiffs [the Catholic Charities family service agencies] under the HRA [Human Rights Act] for refusing to engage in conduct forbidden by their faith undeniably imposes a substantial burden on their religious exercise."[11] —From a legal brief filed in support of the Illinois Catholic Charities family service agencies

choices of where to go for desired services. The unspoken assumption seemed to be that religion and religious claims had no place in the realm of government grants and contracts. Officials making this assumption did not see that religious freedom was infringed upon when public policies did not accommodate themselves to sincerely held religious beliefs. The state never felt the need to consider the religious freedom claims the faith-based agencies put forward.

At the very least, the religious freedom claims of the Illinois faith-based family service agencies should have been evaluated by the standards established in the Religious Freedom Restitution Act (RFRA). As seen earlier, government may not "substantially" burden the free exercise of religion unless it does so to further "a compelling state interest" and achieves this by the least restrictive means. Clearly, the requirement to place children with same-sex and unmarried heterosexual couples imposed a substantial burden on those agencies' free exercise of religion and, given other agencies' willingness to provide such services, one would be hard-pressed to argue Illinois attempted to achieve its public policy goal by the least restrictive means available to it.

Chapter 3 also considered the University of Notre Dame and Wheaton College and the Department of Health and Human Services (HHS) mandate requiring their health care policies to provide contraceptive services that were broadly defined to include what many view as abortifacients. Again, it was an instance of a government policy requiring faith-based institutions to act contrary to their religious beliefs. Here also, principled pluralism says that policies such as the HHS contraceptive mandate should contain an exemption for religiously based organizations with sincere, well-established objections to the policy. From the beginning the mandate exempted religious congregations and their integrated auxiliaries. There is no reason it could not have done the same for religiously based colleges and universities such as Notre Dame and Wheaton. The provisions of RFRA would seem to require this. A substantial burden was being placed on these institutions, and there were less restrictive means by which the government's goal of more widely available contraceptives could have been achieved.

Not wishing to grant a simple exemption, HHS has tried to accommodate the religious beliefs of institutions such as Notre Dame and Wheaton by a series of evolving, complex, round-about mechanisms. But both of these institutions—and many others with similar, religiously based objections to the mandate—understandably believe it still leaves them complicit in the provision of contraceptives and abortifacients. HHS's refusal to grant an exemption to the mandate in the case of religiously rooted colleges and universities and other faith-based organizations as it did for religious congregations reveals a hidden assumption: these faith-based organizations are not truly religiously based, or at the least are not as fully religious as religious congregations. The belief seems to be that not to grant them an exemption poses no real religious freedom problem since they are not fully or truly religious institutions. Freedom of worship was protected, but freedom of religion was not.

For true, comprehensive religious freedom to prevail, however, its protections must extend beyond religious congregations to the full range of religiously based organizations, including educational institutions, hospitals and other health service agencies, social service organizations, and more.

It would be equally a violation of principled pluralism for Notre Dame, Wheaton, or other faith-based organizations with religious

"[HHS has] a host of obvious alternatives for furthering its interest in expanding contraceptive coverage. Any of these alternatives would avoid any need to conscript religious objectors into providing these drugs and services against their consciences."[12] —From Wheaton College's Memorandum of Law in Support of Motion for Preliminary Injunction in *Wheaton College v. Sebelius*

objections to the HHS contraceptive mandate to try to prevent contraceptives from being widely available to the public. In fact both Notre Dame and Wheaton in their legal complaints make clear they have no such intent. They have no intention of trying to prevent the government from making contraceptives freely available through some distribution program of its own. The issue is not the availability of contraceptives, since no one is arguing that individuals be denied access to them. It is not a matter of these institutions seeking to impose their version of a Christian worldview on everyone. It is HHS that is promoting greater uniformity and less choice; Notre Dame and Wheaton are supporting a pluralist view of society with greater diversity and choice.

We also recounted in chapter 3 the failure of HHS to renew a contract with the Catholic bishops (USCCB) that involved providing help to victims of human trafficking. In keeping with Catholic beliefs, the USCCB required agencies with whom it subcontracted not to provide contraceptive and abortion services. A federal District Court decision held that giving a contract to the USCCB under these terms was an unconstitutional establishment of religion. Here also our view of faith-based organizations' religious freedom calls for a respect for religious beliefs, including the right of an organization such as the USCCB to dispense the money it receives in keeping with its religious beliefs and standards. Receiving government money does not turn a faith-based organization—nor a secular nonprofit organization—into an arm

"Through this lawsuit, Notre Dame does not seek to impose its religious beliefs on others. It simply asks that the government not impose its values and policies on Notre Dame, in direct violation of its religious beliefs."[13] —From the complaint filed by the University of Notre Dame in *University of Notre Dame v. Sebelius* in the United States District Court for the Northern District of Indiana

or branch of the government so that its policies must mirror those required of government itself.

The standard for awarding grants should be the quality and effectiveness of the services the organizations competing for the grants will provide; religiously inspired practices should make it neither easier nor harder to obtain government grants. All principled pluralism asks for is a level playing field. Recall that the professional staff at HHS had ranked the USCCB, based on its track record and proposal, as the superior proposal. That is what should count, not preconceived standards banning religiously rooted practices. Doing so puts faith-based organizations at a government-created disadvantage.

All agencies receiving government grants or contracts do not have to look or act alike. In fact, a diversity of practices is a plus. As different organizations follow somewhat different approaches to meeting needs, persons seeking help have more choice and program administrators can learn what approaches are most effective.

Last, there is the chapter 4 case study of the for-profit company Hobby Lobby and its faith-based refusal to provide what its owners see are abortifacients as a part of its health care policy for its employees. Under principled pluralism privately owned, for-profit businesses whose owners are seeking to follow their faith in their business practices should qualify for exemptions from government regulations that they find would require them to violate their beliefs. From the point of view of religious freedom, the key question is not the legal form of an organization—whether it is incorporated or unincorporated or whether it is nonprofit or for-profit—but the existence and nature of the religious commitments that infuse it.

Admittedly, only a small minority of for-profit businesses declare their religious nature by way of mission statements and established practices. Also, the corporate form of business makes possible very large structures where it becomes less likely they will be infused with religious goals and values. Nevertheless, it is the presence or absence of religious goals and values permeating the organization that is important, not incorporated versus unincorporated or nonprofit versus for-profit legal forms.

Hobby Lobby is a good example of where the religious character and purposes of the firm with which its owners infused it should be the key factor, not its corporate and for-profit status. As seen in chapter 4, although Hobby Lobby is incorporated, its owners, the Green family, are directly and intimately involved in running it and have long demonstrated their attempts to practice their evangelical faith in their business. Their position is clearly sincere and rooted in their religious faith. Nor was Hobby Lobby seeking to impose its owners' religious views onto their employees or other businesses. They are only asking to be left alone to follow their beliefs.

Thus, we believe the Supreme Court was right when it applied the standards of RFRA and concluded that the government had not attempted to achieve its goals by the least restrictive means. It

> "For the first time, all schools and community-based organizations—public, nonprofit, for-profit, *faith-based* and charter—were invited to apply. Our sole focus was on finding and funding those programs that work."[14] —Rahm Emanuel, mayor of Chicago

held that Hobby Lobby must therefore be granted an exemption to the contraceptive mandate as formulated by the Department of Health and Human Services. This means the religious freedom rights of for-profit businesses with clear, explicit religious beliefs and commitments must be taken seriously and weighed; it also means those rights will not always prevail. This is right and proper.

But Hobby Lobby's victory before the Supreme Court is no cause for complacency. The court reached its decision by a thin five-to-four majority and was met by a storm of criticism by many in the media and in academic circles. There is no guarantee other for-profit firms will find their religious freedoms protected by the courts.

When Public Policy Got It Right

We close this chapter with an example of where the policy-making process got it right, although the story is not yet complete. This is a positive, if imperfect, example of how people and organizations with very different convictions can live together and find solutions to seemingly intractable issues, even though both sides may view the solution as less than ideal. Our example is the Employment Nondiscrimination Act (ENDA) that was passed by the Senate in November 2013, although it subsequently failed in the House of Representatives.[15] ENDA would have been the first federal law to ban employment discrimination on the bases of sexual orientation and gender identity.

The bill was controversial. Many in and out of government are convinced that it is past time to ban job discrimination against LGBT people. At the same time, many faith-based organizations are based in religious traditions that believe those involved in sexual relations outside of heterosexual marriage are violating God's will for human beings. They do not exclude a person from a job simply because of the person's sexual orientation, but they do require all staff to follow their sexual conduct code. Such organizations understandably believe that hiring staff who are living in violation of the organizations' religious beliefs would undermine their religious nature and witness.

Recognizing the deep convictions of many religions about homosexual conduct, the ENDA bill adopted by the Senate included three important protections for the religious freedom of faith-based organizations: (1) it exempted from its new nondiscrimination requirements religious organizations that are free under Title VII of the 1964 Civil Rights Act to consider religion when hiring staff, thus exempting not only houses of worship but also religious charities, hospitals, schools, and other such faith-based organizations; (2) it provided that a religious organization cannot be denied a government grant or contract, license, accreditation, or tax-exempt status because it does not hire people who would not follow its conduct code; and (3) it specifically stated that its purpose is not only to end wrongful job discrimination but also to uphold religious freedom. The latter two provisions were added to the bill on the Senate floor by an amendment proposed by Senator Rob Portman (R-Ohio).

Some defenders of organizational religious freedom considered the bill still to be flawed; they were not convinced that a bill such as this is the way wrongful job discrimination should be ended. We also believe that ideally the religious freedom protections for faith-based organizations should be stronger. Meanwhile, some gay rights advocates also believed the bill to be flawed, and in fact many gay rights and civil rights organizations pressed hard to eliminate the exemption for faith-based organizations. Some withdrew their support for the bill because of the religious freedom protections that were in it. Many gay rights advocacy organizations are not supporting similar legislation in the new Congress that convened in 2015, but instead are pressing for what is sometimes called a comprehensive LGBT civil rights law.[16]

Nevertheless, we believe that in today's political setting, the Senate ENDA bill provided an acceptable, common-ground solution to a very contentious dispute. Faith-based organizations of a wide variety of types—not just religious congregations—would have been protected from being required or pressured into practices that run counter to their beliefs; LGBT persons would have been protected from arbitrary discrimination where the employer is not a religious organization with a religiously grounded conduct standard.

Similarly, in 2015 the Utah legislature, with the support of the Mormon Church leadership, passed legislation providing civil rights protections for LGBT people, but with religious freedom protections for faith-based organizations, legislation that was welcomed by both religious leaders and LGBT advocates.[17]

These examples illustrate much of what this chapter—indeed much of what this book—is about. In chapter 1 already we called for a renewed commitment to religious freedom, pluralism, and tolerance. To achieve these goals, those concerned with the religious freedom rights of faith-based organizations should attempt to accommodate the public policy goals of those advancing new public policies that threaten their religious freedom; those advancing the new public policies should be willing to accommodate the concerns of those with fears for their religious freedom. For this to occur, there needs to be a rebirth of tolerance and a recommitment from all of us to live together with our differences.

8

Five Questions

★

Both of us over the years have dealt with issues involving organizations' religious freedom. We have written widely, spoken to various groups, and have been interviewed by reporters. In doing so, more than once we have been confronted somewhat angrily by a question that goes something like this: "Will not the religious freedom you are advocating mean religious organizations will be able to engage in all kinds of discrimination against persons or beliefs they don't like?" Less often, persons who tend to agree with us on religious freedom issues will politely ask us something like this: "Doesn't your belief in religious freedom for all religious and even irreligious organizations deny the truth of your Christian beliefs? If all beliefs are treated the same and equally respected, aren't you saying all beliefs are equally valid?"

Questions such as these deserve honest, straightforward answers. This is what we do in this chapter by responding to five questions that are often asked. As we do so, we hope to clarify further our positions on religious freedom for faith-based organizations and the real-world applications of our views.

Are the Religious Freedoms and the Pluralism We Advocate Based in Relativism?

We have called for public policies that protect the rights of adherents and organizations of all religions to live lives consistent with their various faiths. And we do the same for nonreligious, secular persons and their organizations. This may lead some to believe that we are advancing a position rooted in a relativism that says all beliefs—whether religiously based or secular, whether traditionally held or newly minted—are equally sound. Relativism says one person ought not to judge another person's beliefs and practices, since truth resides in the individual. Therefore, all beliefs should be protected in the public realm because what is truth for me may or may not be truth for you. In this view, equal respect for all beliefs rests in their equal validity.

However, the pluralism we advocate—what we have labeled principled pluralism—does not rest on the conviction that the beliefs and practices of all persons and organizations have equal validity or worth. Nor is it rooted in an assumption that all beliefs are true for their holders and thus one ought not to judge among them. As Christians, both of us hold to the truths that have been held and advanced by the church for some two thousand years. We believe they are absolute and hold for all persons, cultures, and times. We desire that more and more persons will come to embrace them. But—and this is crucial—they should do so through winsome examples and persuasion, not by the force of law.

"We can, and should, respect others' duty to follow their consciences even as we insist that they're mistaken."[1] —Kevin Hasson, author of *The Right to Be Wrong* and founder of the Becket Fund for Religious Liberty

If the pluralism and resulting religious freedom we support are not rooted in relativism, what *is* their basis? At their heart, they are based on the recognition that society, as a matter of basic fact, is characterized by people and organizations holding to a wide variety of convictions, both religious and secular. A respect for the worth and dignity of all human beings, as well as a desire to live in peace as one society, lead us to defend the freedom of others, including those with whom we have deep differences. That is why principled pluralism insists that one ought not to force one's understanding of truth onto others. Respect and legal protection for the beliefs asserted by differing religious and secular belief systems should be based on our belief in the dignity of all human beings and a respect for our fellow citizens and their conscientious convictions, even when we believe they are wrong. All citizens have the "right to be wrong," as the title of a book by Kevin Hasson, a Roman Catholic believer, has expressed it.[2] Similarly, Tish Harrison Warren expressed it well in what we quoted earlier: "This is the promise of pluralism—that communities can have opposing ideologies, yet not silence one another, but instead learn to live as neighbors and, more radically, as friends."[3]

Closely related to relativism is the idea that all religious differences are inconsequential. This idea asserts that, as we get to know each other, we will find there are many beliefs and values we hold in common, and remaining differences can be ignored or relegated to the background. Tolerance and respect for each other are thereby rooted in the belief that our differences are actually not all that important. The pluralism we advocate, however, is tougher and more difficult than that. The ideal of a diverse nation or community—whether that diversity is rooted in ethnicity, race, sexual orientation, political opinion, or religion—accepts that there are real differences in society and that these differences matter. A true commitment to diversity involves allowing the differing groups present in society the freedom to express and practice their beliefs and to try to convince others to their point of view while living and working together in a spirit of mutual respect. It is not based on the idea that our differences are really not all that consequential and can be ignored as we emphasize what we have in common. Doing so would do violence to our genuine, sincere differences, replacing them with a gray sameness. This means all must defend the right of those with whom they have clear differences to freely maintain and follow their beliefs.

As we have stated throughout this book, we are as committed to advancing the freedom of the faith-based organizations of our fellow Jewish, Muslim, Sikh, and nonbelieving citizens as we are committed to advancing those of our fellow Christians. This commitment emerges out of our respect and even love for our fellow human beings and fellow citizens—not out of a false belief that our differences are not real or do not matter—and out of our conviction it is not government's place to decide for all of us what ultimate truth is.

Does Pluralism Allow Faith-Based Organizations to Discriminate?

In 2009 a *New York Times* editorial criticized President Barack Obama for allowing faith-based organizations receiving government funds to make hiring decisions based on religion. It proclaimed, "Public money should not be used to pay for discrimination."[4] And in 2015 a controversy exploded onto the public scene when Indiana passed a law that was similar to the federal Religious Freedom Restoration Act (RFRA) we have discussed at several points.[5] It was branded an exercise in bigotry and discrimination, major corporations threatened to boycott Indiana, and protesters rallied. The controversy arose because Indiana's RFRA was seen as potentially giving protection to businesses that wished to discriminate against LGBT persons. The Indiana legislature quickly backtracked and amended its newly enacted law. Such accusations of discrimination are far from rare. We have touched on the issue of "discrimination" practiced by faith-based organizations several times earlier in this book, but we need to look at this common complaint more closely.

The starting point for a careful analysis of the claim that protecting the religious freedom of faith-based organizations will lead to discrimination is the fact that there is rational, appropriate discrimination as well as arbitrary, unjustified discrimination. The *New York Times* editorial (the reaction to Indiana's RFRA law) and the questioner we quote at the beginning of this chapter all assumed a crucial adjective modifying "discrimination"—namely, "invidious" or "arbitrary."

No one, of course, would question the right of a hospital in hiring a surgeon to "discriminate" against persons without surgical training. Nor would anyone question the right of a Baptist church that is seeking a pastor to "discriminate" against an unemployed rabbi who might apply. Why do we not consider such hiring conditions by a hospital or a church as not being actual acts of discrimination? Because there is a logical, necessary connection we all recognize between the job to be filled and the qualification in the one case of being a surgeon and in the other of being a Christian in the Baptist tradition. Similarly, if an adoption agency refuses to place a child with a couple with a history of child abuse, we all would commend the agency, not file a discrimination complaint. Again, there is a logical, necessary connection between the agency's decision and its very nature or purpose.

"Discrimination" is not wrongful discrimination if it is based on factors logically connected to an action to be taken or a position to be filled. There is such a thing as the indiscriminate use of nondiscrimination standards!

For faith-based organizations seeking to be true to their faith traditions, religion-related characteristics and patterns of behavior are logically connected to certain actions or certain positions to be filled. When a Catholic college or university, for example, insists on a number of religiously based belief or behavior standards for its faculty members, we should see the same sort of direct connection as in our first two hypothetical examples. There is a long and intellectually distinguished Catholic tradition of learning and scholarship that spans all fields of study. This tradition was nurtured and developed in Catholic institutions of higher education going back more than a thousand years. It should be no surprise that Catholic colleges and universities today carry on that same tradition in various ways and, to do so, some have concluded at least certain faculty members need to be Catholic.

Similarly, an evangelical adoption agency is rooted in a long, biblically based tradition that regards it best for a child to be raised in a stable, married, husband-and-wife family. Unmarried couples living together—whether same-sex or heterosexual—are seen by the evangelical tradition as being outside of God's will for humankind, as are same-sex couples even when married. Thus an evangelical adoption agency would see placing children with such couples as also putting the agency outside of God's will. To it, doing so would be sin. When that agency therefore refuses to place children with a same-sex or cohabiting heterosexual couple, there is a direct, logical connection between its religious beliefs and its actions.

These specific examples—of a Catholic university favoring Catholic faculty in the one case and of an evangelical adoption agency favoring married, husband-wife families in the other—are not acts of arbitrary, irrational bigotry or bias. True, others will disagree with the policies of the Catholic university or the evangelical adoption agency as they have every right to do. But they cannot argue these are arbitrary positions with no logical support. They are positions rooted in ancient religious traditions and defensible in light of those traditions. The logic supporting them may not be as obvious or as widely accepted as choices by a hospital to "discriminate" against non-surgeons in hiring a surgeon, a Baptist church to "discriminate" against rabbis in hiring a pastor, or an

"The interest of society in the enforcement of employment dis-crimination statutes is undoubtedly important. But so too is the interest of religious groups in choosing who will preach their beliefs, teach their faith, and carry out their mission."[6] —Chief Justice John Roberts in the Supreme Court's *Hosanna-Tabor v. EEOC* decision

adoption agency to "discriminate" against child abusers in placing children for adoption. But that does not mean logic is absent. In all of these instances, there is a close link between the position to be filled or the policy being followed and the tradition, character, and mission of the organizations involved.

To argue that nondiscrimination policies may or should force faith-based organizations to violate their sincerely held, religiously based beliefs is to claim that public policies may force religiously based organizations to deny or undermine their own religious character and to act contrary to their beliefs—the very definition of a religious freedom violation. And remember, these organizations are not trying to impose their beliefs onto the rest of society; they are only asking that society not impose their beliefs onto them.

In order not to be misunderstood, we must follow what we just wrote with an additional observation: the religious freedom we advocate does not say that any and all claimed religious beliefs and practices of faith-based organizations must be protected from nondiscrimination policies our nation has enacted. There are limits to what we are advocating. We have made this point earlier, but it is worth emphasizing here. First, the claimed religious beliefs must be sincerely held. They must not be suddenly discovered beliefs, seemingly rooted in an attempt to avoid a law or public policy an organization does not like or finds burdensome.

Second, the Religious Freedom Restitution Act (RFRA) that we described in earlier chapters both protects the religiously based

practices of faith-based organizations and qualifies that protection
so it will not be abused. RFRA says government may not "substantially" burden the free exercise of religion. It then goes on to
provide that government can only restrict religious free exercise
if the law is furthering "a compelling state interest" and does so
by the least restrictive means.[7]

In other words, if a faith-based organization believes a nondiscrimination regulation is interfering with its free exercise of
religion, it must demonstrate that the interference with its religious
beliefs and practices is not minor or incidental but "substantial."
Those seeking to compel it nonetheless to obey the nondiscrimination requirement must be able to demonstrate that the requirement is supporting a "compelling state interest," that is, it clearly,
convincingly advances or protects the public good. And they must
demonstrate that the requirement supports the public good by a
means that least restricts or limits that organization's religiously
based policies or practices. There must not be another readily
available means to protect the public welfare without restricting
or limiting the religious freedom of faith-based organizations.

Under RFRA—appropriately, we believe—the religious freedom
protections for faith-based organizations are strong and enforce-
able, but they are not absolute. All faith-based organizations are
not exempt from all nondiscrimination laws or regulations they
claim interfere with their religious freedom. Instead, RFRA creates a balancing or weighing process. That process is rightly tilted
in favor of religious freedom. Those claiming that faith-based
organizations must obey a certain nondiscrimination regulation
that interferes with their religious freedom have a high bar they
must clear. But faith-based organizations can be required to obey
nondiscrimination regulations if those regulations significantly
promote the public good and there are no other, less restrictive
means by which to achieve this goal.

Nevertheless, some will find it hard to step back and allow
religiously based organizations the freedom to engage in acts

they view as unjust discrimination. This was all too amply demonstrated by the 2015 controversy over Indiana's RFRA law. We all find it is easy to nod our heads in agreement when someone writes about toleration, respect for those with whom we disagree, and diversity. But where all of us are tested on whether we truly believe in pluralism and the resulting diversity is when we are asked to accept and protect the rights of those with whom we disagree. It is hard for some gay rights activists not to see a Catholic or evangelical adoption agency that refuses to place children with same-sex couples—even married same-sex couples—as engaging in invidious discrimination that must be stopped. It is equally hard for some Catholics and evangelicals to come to the defense of a gay rights activist who has been fired from his job with a secular organization due to his activism. Much of the controversy over Indiana's RFRA law might have been avoided if its religious communities had come together to pass nondiscrimination legislation that protected LGBT persons when religious freedom was not at issue. Principled pluralism insists that what both sides may find hard is exactly what must be done.

It will take an especially strong commitment to pluralism, diversity, and tolerance for those in support of same-sex marriage to accommodate those religious organizations that continue to view a same-sex marriage as not a true marriage from their religious point of view—and for those with religious objections to same-sex marriage to accommodate same-sex couples whenever their religious beliefs will allow them to do so. But we as a society have largely achieved this sort of accommodation in the highly contentious case of legalized abortion; we are hopeful our society can also do so in the case of same-sex marriage.

As a final observation, we cannot think of instances where a faith-based organization could qualify for an exemption from nondiscrimination laws and regulations protecting racial and ethnic minorities. The sincerity test and the RFRA standards offer ample basis for policy makers and courts not to grant faith-based

"Both same-sex couples and religious dissenters face the problem that what they experience as among the highest virtues is condemned by others as a grave evil. Where same-sex couples see loving commitment of mutual care and support, many religious believers see disordered conduct that violates natural law and scriptural command. And where those religious believers see obedience to a loving God who undoubtedly knows best when he lays down rules for human conduct many supporters of gay rights see intolerance, bigotry, and hate."[8] —Marc Stern, General Council, American Jewish Committee; Thomas Berg, Professor, University of St. Thomas School of Law; and Douglas Laycock, Professor, University of Virginia School of Law.

organizations exemptions from such laws and regulations. In terms of the sincerity test, one has to look long and hard today to find a faith-based organization with any sort of claim to exemptions from racial and ethnic nondiscrimination standards based on sincerely held religious beliefs. And if one could find such an organization, it would have to demonstrate under RFRA that there are other ways for government to achieve the nondiscrimination goals that are less restrictive of its religious freedom—a task that would be extremely difficult, if not impossible.

Does Principled Pluralism Allow Organizations to Use Religion as an Excuse to Avoid Laws They Do Not Like?

"There are quite a number of medical treatments that different religious groups object to. So one religious group could opt out of this and another religious group could opt out of that and everything would be piecemeal and nothing would be uniform."[9] This observation by Supreme Court Justice Elena Kagan raises the question to which we respond here: Does principled pluralism allow organizations to use religion as an excuse to avoid valid laws they do not like and thereby destroy or weaken the goals of those laws? This question is similar to the one we just considered but raises a more general concern beyond that of nondiscrimination.

It is a legitimate concern. When we as a community or a society decide on a new public policy through our elected representatives and the normal decision-making process, we have in effect judged that the new policy is for the good of society as a whole. Even those who dissent from the wisdom of the new policy are expected to adhere to it until they can win repeal of it or modifications in it. That is the democratic system that has served us well for over two hundred years.

In light of this some may object, as did Justice Kagan, that if we allow religion-based exemptions to a validly enacted policy, we will undercut the policy and block society from realizing the good the new policy was intended to achieve. In a democracy once society has decided on a new policy, everyone must go along with it, even when we believe it is misguided. If everyone can decide which laws to obey and ignore, an orderly, peaceful society from which we all benefit will be lost.

Our basic response is threefold. First, experience teaches us that providing exemptions for faith-based organizations to enacted laws does not undermine the effective implementation of those laws. As seen earlier, Title VII of the Civil Rights Act of 1964 includes an exemption so that congregations and other religious organizations can consider religion when making employment decisions. It has served us well for fifty years. When we had a military draft, an exemption was provided for religion-based pacifists without threatening the safety of the country. When the Supreme Court in 1973 made abortion legal in almost all cases, conscience clause legislation was quickly passed that protected health professionals and organizations from having to participate in providing abortions. In all these instances, the implementation and effectiveness of the public policy and its goals were not affected in a major way.

History teaches that we can enact what society deems desirable new public policies while at the same time protecting the religious freedom rights of persons and organizations that dissent from the new policy for religious reasons.

It is important to keep in mind that we are considering faith-based *organizations* and their religion-based exemptions from certain legal requirements, not individuals who might claim a religion-based exemption. It is easier to think of examples where individuals might claim a law or regulation requires them to act contrary to their religious beliefs. For example, there have been instances where individual Jehovah Witnesses, true to their religious beliefs, have refused blood transfusions for themselves or their children. There have also been some parents who have refused, on religious grounds, vaccinations for themselves or their children. But we know of no organizations, such as hospitals or health clinics, that have refused to give blood transfusions or inoculations on religious grounds.

Second, as in the case of religion-based exemptions from non-discrimination requirements, there is RFRA and its provisions. If a situation would arise where the welfare of the public at large is threatened by granting organizations religion-based exemptions, and if there are no other means available to provide for the public welfare that are less restrictive of the religious freedom of faith-based organizations, RFRA would allow such restrictions. And we agree it should. A possible instance would be a religious sect that refuses inoculations for a highly communicable disease, thereby threatening attempts to stop the disease from spreading among the general population. Its schools or other organizations—assuming it has such—could be required to take part in an inoculation program.

Third, principled pluralism advocates religion-based exemptions for faith-based organizations only when they are based on sincerely held religious beliefs. This also limits the possibility of the abuse of religion-based exemptions. Religious beliefs are obviously sincere when they are rooted in known religious traditions going back hundreds, if not thousands, of years. We are thinking of religious traditions such as Judaism, Roman Catholicism, evangelical Protestantism, Islam, Sikhism, and Native American religion. The religious beliefs and practices of faith-based organizations that are based in new or more recent religious movements should also be protected by exemptions as long as they can demonstrate their beliefs are sincere, and not attempts to evade a law and its requirements. In cases of individual persons, courts have been called to make this distinction between sincere religious claims versus attempts to evade some law or regulations; they can also do so in the case of organizations.

Are Faith-Based Organizations Really as Equally Religious as Congregations?

It is easy to assume that religious congregations are religious in a deeper, fuller, more direct way than faith-based service organizations, which are active in the public worlds of education, health care, and social services. Consequently, it is easy to conclude faith-based organizations do not have religious freedom rights or, if they do, these rights are more limited than those of churches and other religious congregations, something we have denied throughout this book.

We acknowledge that religious congregations, with their worship services, prayers, rituals, and celebrations, are religious in a different way than religiously based health clinics, K–12 schools, colleges, overseas development agencies, spouse abuse shelters, and other such entities. When a health clinic provides free flu shots, a K–12 school teaches children to read, a college teaches calculus, an overseas development agency provides microloans to persons starting their own businesses, or a domestic abuse shelter provides refuge and help to a woman who has been cruelly treated, they appear to be less engaged in religious acts than religious congregations.

But it is important to dig beneath surface appearances. When one does, one sees that, while the various actions we used in the above examples are religious in a different way than a congregation's prayers and rituals, for the faithful they are equally religious in character. It is a matter of difference, not a matter of degree. Recall the quotations of Pope Benedict XVI and Richard Stearns we highlighted in chapter 1. These representatives of the two largest faith traditions in the United States insist that public acts of mercy and care are an integral part of the gospel. The ancient Hebrew prophet Isaiah at one point surprisingly railed against and condemned the Hebrews' religious festivals, prayers, and celebrations. Why? Because the Hebrew people were not pursuing justice and mercy (Isa. 1:10–17). Similarly, one of the Five Pillars of Islam—one of the five primary duties of religiously observant Muslims—is *zakat*, that is, charity or social responsibility, which is "considered part of one's service to God."[10]

The key point is not merely that acts of mercy and caring for others are important for people of faith. Instead, it is that such acts are *as essential to the faith* as the more traditionally and easily recognized religious acts of worship and prayer. They are different but no less central or important.

Nonbelievers may think this strange and scratch their heads, but no one can deny that this is what Christian, Jewish, Muslim, and other religious traditions believe. For persons outside those traditions to insist that they know better is itself a sign of intolerance and violates religious freedom.

There is a second consideration. As we noted earlier in chapter 2, religious believers and their organizations often engage in acts of education, healing, and help in ways different from secular persons and organizations. People of religious conviction typically approach their humanitarian and educational work in the context of certain religiously based ideas or worldviews. The basis for human dignity and worth, perspectives on procreation, seeing the hand of God in the regularities of mathematics, recognizing the equal dignity of all human beings, and views concerning the nature of the family and other human communities—all these and much, much more are examples of religiously rooted perspectives and values that help shape how religiously based schools, health centers, and social service agencies go about their work. True, they are engaged in humanitarian work, but their religiously based beliefs and values shape how they do that work. Because of this, their supposedly "secular" humanitarian and educational activities are in fact shaped by—are imbued with—their religious beliefs and values.

Does Religious Freedom Violate the Separation of Church and State?

Some believe the protection of the religious freedom rights of faith-based organizations we advocate in this book leads to the violation of the separation of church and state. Under principled pluralism and the resulting religious freedoms—as we have developed and explained them in this book—faith-based organizations would be exempt from various nondiscrimination laws that clash with their beliefs, even when they may receive part of their funding from government grants or contracts. Similarly, some faith-based organizations would be free not to engage in certain practices that run counter to their religiously based beliefs, while their secular counterparts would be required to engage in those practices. Religiously based student organizations could benefit from meeting on campus, posting notices on campus bulletin boards, and sometimes sharing in university funds.

Some argue that in all these instances religion is being helped or supported by public policies. And that, in their thinking, violates the separation of church and state. Does not the First Amendment erect a wall of separation between church and state? How then, they contend, can tax dollars go to support faith-based organizations and their activities, particularly when those organizations may be exempt from some requirements that apply to secular organizations? In the prior section and throughout the book we have made the case that many faith-based organizations are religious in a profound and deep manner. We argued they are as religious as religious congregations and their worship activities. How then can we turn around and advocate government support and accommodation for these organizations, support and accommodation that clearly benefit them?

Our answer is that the religious freedom we advocate does not seek special or favored treatment for any religion's educational, health care, and social service organizations, nor for faith-based organizations generally. Faith-based educational and service organizations should be treated no worse—and no better—than their secular counterparts. Equal treatment, not favored treatment, is our goal. And that is what the religious freedom language of the First Amendment requires.

Think what would result if faith-based organizations could not share in the benefits and government programs that secular organizations of a similar nature receive. Or if they could do so only if they abandoned their religious beliefs and standards. That would mean government, by its policies, would be putting faith-based organizations at a government-created disadvantage. Secular overseas relief and development agencies could receive government grants; faith-based ones could not—or could only if they surrendered much of their religious character. Public policies could require faith-based health clinics, in violation of their religious beliefs, to deliver the same services in the same way as secular health clinics. Similarly, government regulations could require public-serving faith-based organizations to go against their religious traditions' beliefs in such areas as the standards for their employees and the services they offer. Many of the religious freedom violations we have presented in this book have been of this nature—denying benefits to faith-based organizations that their secular counterparts receive or trying to squeeze them into a secular mold.

"[The Constitution's] Religion Clauses require government to minimize the extent to which it either encourages or discourages religious belief or disbelief, practice or nonpractice, observance or nonobservance. . . . [Religion] should proceed as unaffected by government as possible."[11] —Douglas Laycock, professor of law, University of Virginia

When faith-based organizations experience religious freedom violations, the end result is that they suffer government-created disadvantages. Government rules and regulations would make it harder for them to follow their religious beliefs and practices. Government would no longer be treating religious organizations in a neutral, evenhanded manner but would be imposing disadvantages onto them that their secular counterparts do not have to endure.

Principled pluralism, as we have advocated it here, supports government neutrality—defined as evenhandedness or equal treatment—on matters of religion. A true understanding of the separation of church and state means government, through its policies, should not favor any one religion over another nor favor secular beliefs and organizations over religious ones—nor religious beliefs or organizations over secular ones. It should not advantage or disadvantage any religious tradition over others, nor either religion as a whole or secular beliefs as a whole.

The Supreme Court in its church-state decisions has wavered in its interpretations, but there is a clear line of decisions that supports our understanding of religious freedom and the separation of church and state. For example, Justice Anthony Kennedy wrote the following in a majority decision of the Court:

> A central lesson of our [prior] decisions is that a significant factor in upholding governmental programs in the face of Establishment Clause attack is their neutrality towards religion. . . . We have held

that the guarantee of neutrality is respected, not offended, when
the government, following neutral criteria and evenhanded policies,
extends benefits to recipients whose ideologies and viewpoints,
including religious ones, are broad and diverse.[12]

In this line of reasoning—which has often been used by the Court—
government religious neutrality is violated when it refuses religiously based, public-serving organizations government benefits
that their secular counterparts receive. It is also violated when
government pressures faith-based organizations to violate their
religiously based practices and become more like their secular
counterparts. Instead, government neutrality is achieved by treating
religiously based and secular organizations evenhandedly; neither
one nor the other is to be treated better or worse. That is what
principled pluralism and the religious freedoms it supports ask,
nothing more and nothing less.

We have, of course, not been able to consider here all of the
actual and potential questions people can and have raised concerning the pluralism and religious freedom we are advocating in this
book. It is our hope that the five we have been able to consider
help to clarify the nature and limits of the pluralism we advance
in this book and the thinking that supports it.

9

Religious Freedom Supports
the Common Good

Three Non-Christian Voices

★

Both of us come from Christian backgrounds, and the three "Interlude" essays we have included are also written by persons coming from Christian backgrounds—Catholic and evangelical. Religious freedom, however, is much, much more than a Christian concern. Religious freedom benefits all faiths and society as a whole, and people of various faith commitments or philosophical positions can and do support religious freedom and its robust practice. The concerns we have expressed in this book for the religious freedom of organizations, as well as the principled pluralism and its applications we have discussed, are not narrowly Christian in nature. They support the common good, not merely the "Christian good."

Therefore, to help give life to this broad view of religious freedom and the pluralism that respects persons and organizations of all faiths and of none, this chapter presents three essays written by persons coming from three different non-Christian backgrounds:

an Orthodox Jew, two Muslim scholars, and a legal scholar writing from a nonreligious, or secular, perspective.

They help demonstrate that the commitment to religious freedom, pluralism, and tolerance we first called for at the beginning of chapter 1, and that we have sought to elaborate and defend throughout this book, indeed protects the rights of all faiths, and thereby supports the welfare of society as a whole—the common good.

Protecting Religious Freedom for All Guarantees It to All— Nathan Diament

"Can it happen here, in America?" When all else is stripped away, that is the lens through which Jewish Americans—especially Orthodox Jewish Americans—look at issues associated with religious liberty in the United States. Are the guarantees, both legal and cultural, of religious liberty and pluralism in the nation strong enough and broad enough to allow Jews to hold our beliefs and practice our rituals without interference . . . or persecution?

American Jews realize that the religious freedom our faith community has enjoyed in the United States is unprecedented in the millennia of global Jewish history. The American Jewish experience of liberty, compared to Jewish experiences elsewhere, is not merely a "difference of degree"; it is a fundamental "difference in kind."

For thousands of years, Jews were persecuted in Europe, the Middle East, and elsewhere at the hands of Christians, Muslims, and atheist despots. The only "right" a Jew could hope for over centuries of history was to be left alone and not killed in a pogrom.

In time, where Jews were afforded some basic rights, it was in a mode of "toleration" by the majority religion or the ruling regime. Enlightenment France granted basic rights to Jews, but with the clear cultural understanding that one may be "a Jew in the home, but a Frenchman in the street."

The United States of America, at its inception, offered an entirely new experience of religious liberty for Jews and anchored its guarantee in its constitutional architecture. Perhaps the most concise presentation of this revolutionary promise is to be found in the famous letter written in 1790 by President George Washington to the Jewish community of Newport, Rhode Island. Washington states,

> The citizens of the United States of America have a right to applaud themselves for having given to mankind examples of an enlarged and liberal policy—a policy worthy of imitation. All possess alike liberty of conscience and immunities of citizenship. It is now no more that toleration is spoken of as if it were the indulgence of one class of people that another enjoyed the exercise of their inherent natural rights, for, happily, the Government of the United States, which gives to bigotry no sanction, to persecution no assistance, requires only that they who live under its protection should demean themselves as good citizens in giving it on all occasions their effectual support.

This promise of the full and equal enjoyment of religious liberty was anchored in the nation's new Constitution in two critical ways. One was of course the First Amendment's prohibition of the "establishment" of religion (alongside the guarantee of religious free exercise), but just as important was the prohibition against a "religious test for office."

Many colonial and state constitutions did contain a requirement that elected officials affirm their faith in Jesus and the teachings of the New Testament. Had such a requirement remained in place, the status of Jews and those of other faiths would indeed have been second tier. (This prompted early American Jewish leader Jonas Phillips of Philadelphia to petition the Constitutional Convention to omit such a requirement, and he prevailed.)

While it is certainly true that Jews in America experienced anti-Semitism and discrimination in personal interactions, employment, accommodations, and other realms, the fact that foundationally and structurally Jews were assured of equal rights and status guaranteed its eventual near eradication and a flourishing American Jewish community. Religious Jewish life thrives throughout the United States, and Jews are prominent participants in all sectors of society.

In the politico-cultural realm, Jews have been more than accepted and integrated. While in the last century there was a single "Jewish seat" on the Supreme Court, there was little notice when, with Elena Kagan's nomination, three Jewish justices now sit on the high court. Joe Lieberman's 2000 nomination as the Democrat's vice presidential candidate saw his Orthodox Judaism welcomed in political circles as an asset. President George W. Bush commenced, and President Obama has continued, an annual gala White House Hanukkah Reception at which I've often noted that centuries ago, heads of state were not throwing (kosher catered) Hanukkah parties for their Jewish populations—an invitation to the palace was dreaded!

But Jews are acutely aware in our own minds that we are a minority faith in the United States. Moreover, Orthodox Judaism is a minority of a minority. So we remain watchful and vigilant of the scope of religious freedom available for us and for adherents of other faiths.

Judaism is not only a religion of beliefs; we are required to engage in an array of religious ritual practices including Sabbath observance, *brit milah* (circumcision), keeping a kosher diet, differentiated gender roles within the synagogue, and many more. We are aware that these practices are minority practices, and we are witnessing, particularly in contemporary Europe, renewed campaigns to stigmatize and outlaw many of these fundamental faith practices.

Alongside Judaism's demands for religious ritual practices, Judaism places comprehensive obligations upon how a Jew conducts his business dealings, interpersonal relationships, and all other aspects of life. A quarter of the volumes of the *Shulchan Aruch* (*Code of Jewish Law*) are devoted to the laws and ethics of business and other interpersonal dealings. Judaism recognizes no notion of "being a Jew in the home" and something else in the street or office or classroom or marketplace or park.

And so this brings many of us back to the question of "can it happen here?" Our belief and experience in the United States suggests not, but we can only wonder whether a cultural tide can swell and the ability of Jews to practice our faith not only in our homes but also in our institutions could be curtailed.

Therefore, we ally ourselves with those who fight for the most expansive view of religious liberty. A view that ensures such liberty to individuals and institutions, especially those whose faith-informed views may not be popular but are nonetheless protected. Only through a commitment to religious pluralism and legal protections from religion-informed beliefs and actions being interfered with by the state, can we ensure that all are free to believe and practice their faith in the United States.

Nathan Diament is the executive director for Public Policy of the Union of Orthodox Jewish Congregations of America.

Divine Command, Freedom, and the Common Good— Hamza Yusuf Hanson and Mahan Hussain Mirza

Historically, Islamic civilization has always been a multiethnic, multilingual, and multireligious entity spanning at one point from the Iberian Peninsula to the Malay Archipelago. Muslims today proudly appeal to their premodern past to highlight these facts: after emigration to Medina in the year 622 CE, because of a decade of severe persecution in his hometown of Mecca, the Prophet Muhammad drafted a constitution that recognized believers and nonbelievers as being members of a single community; upon the

bloodless conquest of Jerusalem less than two decades later, the
caliph Umar preserved the sanctity of the Church of the Holy
Sepulcher for Christians by forbidding Muslims to worship inside; for centuries from Samarkand to Seville, scholars—Jewish,
Christian, Muslim, Arab, Persian, pagan—collaborated in the
pursuit of scientific knowledge; the Ottomans permitted religious
communities the right to self-govern according to their respective
laws, customs, and religious teachings in semiautonomous political
units known as millets. Moreover, although it is well known that
the Ottomans gave refuge to Jews fleeing the Spanish Inquisition
in the fifteenth century, it is less known that the first proclamation
of religious tolerance in Europe, the Edict of Torda in sixteenth
century Hungary, was arguably a direct result of Ottoman political
and cultural influence.

Considered rationally, the command to submit to God's will—
literally *Islam*—with the promise of reward for obedience and
punishment for disobedience, necessitates a concomitant freedom to choose one path or another in order for the consequences
to be meaningful. Although the history of Islamic thought is as
diverse as the lands and geographies in which it developed, Muslims have typically understood and embraced this freedom, or
perhaps responsibility, with an overwhelming majority adhering
to a theology of "voluntarism" or "divine command." According
to this perspective, things are good or virtuous simply because
God has commanded them, not because they are good essentially.

It should be clear that theological voluntarism is not antithetical to reason, and the jurisprudential tradition that has operated
within the framework of divine command has always upheld these
higher objectives as axiomatic: the preservation of life and the
intellect, religious freedom, family bonds, wealth and property,
and human dignity. No doubt the detailed understanding of these
principles has shifted over time, but the fact that these lie at the
core of the Muslim legal tradition is undeniable. It has, therefore,
rightly been argued by modern Muslim scholars that the rights and

protections accorded to Muslims under the Constitution of the United States are in harmony with these objectives. In America, Muslims have always had the freedom to submit to God as they have understood him and his authority through systematic readings of their scriptures. The day that traditional Jews, Christians, Muslims, or members of any faith tradition fear the risk of not mere ostracism or stigma but legal prosecution for their beliefs is a sad day indeed. Secular fundamentalism is no better than religious fundamentalism, and Muslims stand in solidarity with other faith communities to advocate for the right to live and preach their convictions in the public sphere.

Even cursory readings of the Qur'an indicate that "there is no compulsion in religion" and that "the truth is clear from your Lord, so let him who will, believe, and let him who will, disbelieve." It is true that there have been and always will be multiple readings of texts among religious communities, just like there are different interpretations of secular laws and constitutions by jurists on different sides of the aisle. The best way to mediate these differences is not by government overreach where one side is outlawed or where religious organizations and associations are coerced to make unconscionable accommodations but by allowing for a plurality of opinions to engage in free and open debate. Let the power of persuasion rest in arguments, and let the quest for human flourishing lie in a healthy competition among institutions—secular and religious—for better outcomes for the common good.

The world is in moral decay. There is uncertainty in the financial system. Our security is under threat. The Muslim world, in particular, is ablaze. Apart from the horrific and enduring consequences of colonialism, ongoing occupation, a gluttonous and tyrannical cultural and political elite, and civil war, as we speak, Christian communities that have always found protection and have flourished in Muslim heartlands are under threat. By building successful faith-based institutions in America, we hope that our efforts will be a model and bring hope and relief not just to Muslims everywhere but also to all lawful citizens in Muslim lands. If the good faith efforts of Muslim American institutions are thwarted due to laws that make their operation untenable on religious grounds, it would be a travesty with untold consequences for all.

Hamza Yusuf Hanson is president of Zaytuna College, and Mahan Hussain Mirza is the dean at Zaytuna College, the only Muslim liberal arts college in the United States.

Religious Liberty for All Is a Secular Liberal Value— Douglas Laycock

Christianity quit making sense to me at about age fourteen, and the older I get, and the longer I think about it, the more unattractive and unbelievable it seems. If an omnipotent being is going to punish me eternally for finding Christianity unbelievable, then I'm in deep trouble. But that possibility, which of course is nonfalsifiable, does not make me any more able to believe.

Politically, I believe in personal liberty *and* in personal responsibility in the exercise of that liberty, in the power of economic incentives *and* in a strong social safety net *and* in helping every child to the starting line of equal opportunity. That combination of positions puts me on the center-left of the political spectrum and in deep disagreement with many conservative Christians on issues of personal liberty and economic policy. Yet I have devoted much of my career to defending the religious liberty of conservative Christians and of other religious groups whose faith claims seem just as implausible. Why is a thoroughly secular liberal deeply committed to religious liberty?

I am committed to religious liberty because I remain true to secular liberalism's fundamental principles, which respect and protect human differences. I support strong protection for the free exercise of religion for the same reasons that I support strong protection against government establishment of religion, strong protection of freedom of speech, and strong protection of the right to control our own sex lives and our own reproduction. Human liberty is a good thing, and especially so with respect to matters that are deeply personal. We should let every American live his own life by his own deepest values—except where government has a compelling reason to interfere.

For many believers and nonbelievers alike, beliefs about religion are fundamental to identity. Some people are willing to die for their faith; some are willing to kill for it. That level of religious commitment has no doubt declined (and a good thing too), but it is still the case that government interference with religious commitments causes human suffering and social conflict.

Believers required to violate their faith may comply with the law and fear that they have ruined or disrupted their relationship with God. Or they may defy the law and incur fines, imprisonment, or loss of government benefits. Or they may escape the reach of the law by surrendering some other right—giving up the business or activity that is subject to the regulation that would require them to violate their religious commitments. Or they may try to violate the law without getting caught—going underground, practicing their religion in secret, and constantly worrying about detection. Each of these possibilities is a bad outcome. Each is a way of coping with the conflict between regulation and deeply held religious commitments; each inflicts its own form of suffering on the victims.

If government inflicts these choices on a group large enough to resist, the inevitable consequence is serious social conflict. We have mostly learned to avoid open violence, although it took a long time to learn that lesson, and much of the world has not learned it yet. And of course government has not surrendered its claim to legitimate violence. Arrest, imprisonment, and even fines depend on whatever violence is necessary to overcome resistance. And while American governments no longer imprison for religious belief, many of them claim the right to fine or imprison for religious practices that violate any law that is said to be "neutral and generally applicable."

Religious liberty is the best means of minimizing these conflicts and these intrusions on personal identity. It is an essential means of enabling people with fundamentally different views on the most important questions to live together in relative peace and equality. To be effective, it must protect the religious beliefs and practices of individuals, of churches and other places of worship, and of faith-based organizations.

My commitment to religious liberty does not depend on the view that religion is good or bad or valuable or harmful, or that one or a few particular religions are any of those things. Religion is clearly a powerful force for good in the lives of many. Equally clearly, it is a powerful force for evil in the lives of many others. But religion's susceptibility to misuse does not distinguish it from any other human institution or belief system. I do not support religious liberty because religion is good but because religion is profoundly important to those who care about it.

In general, religious liberty is good for religion. Religious faith flourishes best when government stays out of the way, interfering neither to deliberately restrict nor to offer its clumsy and often corrupting support. But religious liberty does not mean that the religious side, or the conservative Christian side, should win every lawsuit on every religious liberty issue. Neither does it mean that the secular side, or the antireligious side (not the same, but there are such people), should win every lawsuit. Far too many Americans seem to think one or the other of these things. No matter what the issue, they think religious liberty means that their side should win.

For me, one's views on the truth or value of religion should be wholly irrelevant to one's views on religious liberty. The whole point of religious liberty is that people from across the whole range of views about religion agree to respect the religious liberty of everyone else across the whole range of views about religion. But we aren't there yet. Americans on both sides of the culture wars are far more willing to respect or protect the liberty of people they agree with, and far too eager to minimize or deny the liberty of those they deeply disagree with.

Religious liberty should mean that conservative Christians— and liberal Christians, and Jews and Muslims, and every other faith group, popular or not—are allowed not just to believe their religion but also to practice it, unless they are inflicting significant harm on someone else. Making someone else feel offended, insulted, or irritated is rarely the kind of harm that government has a compelling interest in preventing. Religious liberty should also mean that nonbelievers, Jews, Muslims, and other religious minorities are free to attend government meetings without being subjected to a Christian prayer service, however brief. Many Americans agree with the religious-practice half of this paragraph (or at least that it should apply to religions they approve of) and disagree with the government-prayer half. Many other Americans agree with the government-prayer half and disagree with the religious-practice half. Within each group, these positions are often taken for self-serving reasons. But those who are seriously committed to religious liberty for all should agree with both halves of this paragraph—with full protection for religious practice and with full protection from established religion.

Douglas Laycock is the Robert E. Scott Distinguished Professor of Law and Professor of Religious Studies at the University of Virginia, and Alice McKean Young Regents Chair in Law Emeritus at the University of Texas.

10

How Faith-Based Organizations Can Protect Their Religious Freedom

★

In our experience, faith-based service organizations desire to serve others with excellence and respect—and in a way that reflects and honors the religious convictions that shape their identity as faith-based organizations. And they are rightly concerned about threats to their faith-based practices. But they sometimes fail to take steps that would help protect those practices. For a faith-based organization to sit back, not think through the legal and moral bases of its faith-based practices, ignore emerging threats, and then hit the panic button when suddenly an advocacy group, the media, or a new government regulation undercuts one of its faith-based practices is a recipe for failure and frustration.

We conclude our book, therefore, by presenting five very practical steps that faith-based organizations themselves can take, in a proactive manner, to protect their religious freedom rights.

Principled pluralism and the religious freedoms it protects not only have implications for the public policy and legal interpretations we have already considered, but they also suggest important steps faith-based organizations themselves can take to protect their religious freedom.

Be Explicit in Your Religious Commitments

Some leaders of faith-based organizations understandably fear their religious character may make it more difficult for them to obtain government or private foundation grants, or they may suspect their religious character may make it more difficult to obtain accreditation or needed licenses. Therefore they downplay their religious commitments and practices. They hope to fly under the radar and thereby avoid possible lawsuits or the denial of certain benefits available to similar, nonreligious organizations.

This, however, is the exact wrong approach. It is crucial that religiously based organizations be upfront and explicit in their religious commitments. They need to hold themselves out to the public as being truly religious in nature. The only basis on which faith-based organizations can—and should—receive protections for their distinctive practices is if they can demonstrate those practices are clearly and genuinely embedded in their organization's religious nature. This can be done by way of organizations' mission statements, orientation materials for new employees, words and images on websites, and a well-defined consistency among religious beliefs, organizational policies, and actual practices. It may also be helpful if an organization can demonstrate long-standing ties to a religious tradition, whether that is to a specific church, denomination, or religious body or to a more general religious tradition.

Playing down its religious character might help an organization obtain government grants or contracts or to win accreditation or

certain licenses. However, the bigger challenge faith-based organizations are facing today relates to civil rights laws and other
government regulations and requirements that can pressure them to
act contrary to their religious character. If an organization claims
an exemption from an otherwise valid law or regulation, it must
be able to demonstrate that without the exemption it would be
compelled to violate a religiously based belief rooted in its religious
tradition. But if it has been downplaying its religious character, it
will appear as though it has suddenly created a religious belief or
practice in order to avoid the new law or regulation. Neither the
government nor the public is likely to treat as credible beliefs that
appear to have been discovered just when the organization finds
it convenient to escape a certain legal requirement. This is why it
is important that faith-based organizations be clear and explicit
about their religious character and mission.

Also, being explicit about one's religious character will send
the appropriate signals to persons applying for a job opening
at a faith-based organization or seeking services from it. Such
transparency is not only the appropriate, honest thing to do, but
it will also lessen the possibility of persons feeling they were at-
tracted to a faith-based organization under false pretenses. This
in turn may reduce the chances of complaints or even lawsuits by
disgruntled clients or job applicants who feel they were misled.

Recall the lawsuit World Vision faced after it let three of its
employees go after they no longer agreed with its faith statement.
World Vision was greatly helped by the fact that it had earlier

---

"World Vision's organizing principles were religious, it has always
presented itself as a religious institution, and it continues to do
so."[1] —From the majority opinion in *Spencer v. World Vision*,
holding that World Vision could legally make employment decisions based on religion

adopted a mission statement that clearly and explicitly expressed its religious orientation and commitment. In addition, its formal, announced policies and actual practices were in line with its mission statement. Similarly, Hobby Lobby was helped in winning its case before the Supreme Court by both its mission statement—which makes clear it was founded on Christian principles—and the fact that its faith commitment affects in important ways how it does business. The official opinion of the Court acknowledged that "no one has disputed the sincerity of their religious beliefs."[2] Various Catholic organizations have been helped in court decisions against having to comply with the HHS contraceptive mandate because opposition to the use of contraceptives is a well-established, well-known position of the Catholic Church.

The practical realities of religious freedom in our country make one thing clear: a faith-based organization seeking an exemption from a law or regulation that would weaken its religious character has to be able to demonstrate that its objections are rooted in sincere, serious religious convictions. It thereby protects itself from the charge that the religious exemption it seeks would open the gates for a flood of other exemptions, both legitimate and illegitimate. To claim such protection, the religious organizations themselves must be upfront, clear, and explicit about their religious nature and commitments.

Avoid Even the Appearance of Coercing Others to Follow One's Religiously Based Practices

It is important that faith-based organizations defending their religious freedom rights make a distinction between not being coerced to go against their own religious beliefs and imposing their religious beliefs onto others. This is crucial. The religious freedom standards we have presented throughout this book defend diversity by insisting that faith-based organizations must not be coerced or pressured into going against their religious beliefs; those standards also defend diversity by insisting that faith-based organizations must not seek to coerce or pressure others to follow their religious beliefs. If faith-based organizations are to maintain their credibility in the ongoing and coming debates, it is important to make and live by this distinction.

Those insisting that a faith-based organization must offer certain services to the public even when doing so goes against the religious beliefs of that organization often argue that otherwise the organization is imposing its religious beliefs onto others (those it serves or employs). Claims of theocracy are made. This sort of argument has been made in such cases as a faith-based organization not offering contraceptives in their employees' health insurance, a faith-based hospital not offering abortions or sterilization procedures, and an adoption agency not placing children with same-sex couples. We totally reject that argument. But in doing so we must be clear that we are defending the right of faith-based organizations to be true to their own religious beliefs; we do not defend their trying to coerce others to live by those organizations' religious tenets.

There are two distinctions that faith-based organizations should make in order not to be vulnerable to the charge that they are forcing their religious beliefs onto others in the course of defending their religious freedom. As faith-based organizations successfully make these two distinctions, they will be in a better position to defend their religiously based beliefs and standards. For they will

"Through this lawsuit, Notre Dame does not seek to impose its religious beliefs on others. It simply asks that the government not impose its values and policies on Notre Dame, in direct violation of its religious beliefs."[3] —From the University of Notre Dame's complaint in *University of Notre Dame v. Sebelius*

have made clear they are defending their own religious freedom (which the public and courts are likely to support), not seeking to impose their beliefs onto society as a whole (which few are likely to support).

Before discussing these two distinctions, however, we need to make clear that there are no hard and fast ways that these key distinctions—and the overall goal of not forcing one's beliefs onto others—are to be attained. This admittedly is a difficult area marked by some important but subtle distinctions. We will discuss how the two of us would apply them; others may draw the lines somewhat differently than we do in the examples we use here. And that is fine. What is important, and what we do insist upon, is that religious freedom protections—and the possible exemptions from otherwise existing laws and regulations—must be aimed at protecting genuine religious freedom rights, not coercing or pressuring others to follow one's religious standards.

The first distinction we believe a faith-based organization should make is between providing services to persons it is convinced are engaged in activities that are legal but immoral, and providing services that make it complicit in those immoral activities. In the latter case, providing the services involves the organization in the immoral activity. On the other hand, if a faith-based organization would only offer its services to people who in its view are not engaging in any immoral activities, it would have a very small client base! The very point of many faith-based service organizations is to offer comfort, help, and support in the name of their faith to those who have made wrong choices—including, in their view, sinful choices. In doing so, they have a right not to become complicit in those choices but to show a better way marked by positive choices. The line between serving "sinners" and participating in their "sin" can be hard to draw. But this is an important distinction that all faith-based organizations need to make.

Taking a real-world example, Jonathan and Elaine Huguenin are evangelical Christians who own a photography business in

Albuquerque, New Mexico.[4] When a same-sex couple approached the lead photographer, Elaine Huguenin, to photograph their commitment ceremony, she refused, saying to do so would violate her religious beliefs that same-sex relations are against God's will. She believed that using her artistic abilities to record the ceremony would make her complicit in an activity that her faith had led her to believe was wrong. The same-sex couple brought suit, charging unlawful discrimination. The case went to the New Mexico Supreme Court, and the Huguenins lost. We believe their religious freedom rights were violated.

In this case Elaine Huguenin made an important and proper distinction. As the New Mexico Supreme Court decision stated, "Elane Photography argues that it would have taken portrait photographs and performed other services for same-sex customers, so long as they did not request photographs that involved or endorsed same-sex weddings." Elaine Huguenin was not refusing to provide services to persons she believed were engaged in immoral activities; she was only refusing to provide services that she interpreted as endorsing or supporting an immoral activity. Although the Huguenins lost their case in the New Mexico courts, they made the correct distinction and thereby strengthened their legal case.

The distinction between being complicit in what one views as an immoral activity versus providing goods or services to persons one views as acting immorally will sometimes be a difficult one

"But of course, the Huguenins are not trying to prohibit anyone from marrying. They only want to be left alone to conduct their photography business in a manner consistent with their moral convictions. In their view, they seek only the freedom *not* to endorse someone else's lifestyle."[5] —Justice Richard Bosson from his concurring opinion in *Elane Photography v. Willock*

to make. And two persons may understandably disagree in specific cases where it should be drawn. But we are convinced it is an important distinction faith-based organizations should make.

A second distinction we believe a faith-based organization should make is to distinguish between refusing to provide a service its religious beliefs hold to be immoral and attempting to prevent someone from obtaining that service elsewhere. This is the distinction between, for example, an evangelical adoption agency refusing on religious grounds to place children for adoption with same-sex couples versus that same agency lobbying state regulators to forbid all same-sex adoptions.

In addition, a faith-based organization that believes it cannot in good conscience provide a certain service ought not to be required to refer its clients or patients to other organizations willing to provide that service. Making a referral carries with it the connotation of a recommendation and may even involve arranging an appointment. Some faith-based organizations may be willing to do this, but it is understandable if others decide they cannot, believing doing so would make them complicit in providing the service. One ought not to expect a Catholic hospital that cannot provide an abortion, in keeping with its religious beliefs, to refer the same woman to a nearby abortion clinic. This would make the hospital complicit in the abortion.

The situation becomes murkier, however, when it comes not to making a referral but simply providing information where a certain service can be obtained. In the day of Google and the internet—or simply the Yellow Pages—it is hard to imagine persons who have been denied a certain service not being able to find an alternative provider of that service on their own. But in those instances where a person might be ignorant of the availability of a service elsewhere, we favor providing the information—perhaps even while suggesting morally acceptable alternatives and recommending against going elsewhere to obtain that service. And a faith-based organization refusing a certain service on religious grounds surely ought not to mislead someone into thinking that service is not available elsewhere.

Again, we are in an area of fine distinctions, and some may draw lines somewhat differently than we would. But what we do maintain is that all faith-based organizations whose religious freedom rights allow them to refuse to provide a certain service should make certain they are protecting their own religiously shaped consciences, not trying to block others with different conscientious standards from obtaining that service. As they do so, they will strengthen their ability—and the ability of other faith-based organizations—to resist providing certain goods or services it finds morally unacceptable.

In this section we made two distinctions: between being complicit in what one views as an immoral activity versus merely serving persons engaged in certain activities one views as immoral, and between not offering services that one's religious beliefs forbid one to offer versus trying to block others from receiving that service elsewhere. As faith-based organizations maintain these two distinctions, they will signal their commitment to a truly pluralist public realm and will strengthen their efforts to defend their own religious freedom rights.

Show Respect for and Work with Others Who Disagree with You

A commitment to religious freedom for all entails not only demanding that one's rights be respected but also working for policies that respect the religious or nonreligious convictions of others. This is not only the right thing to do, but it can work to protect one's own religious freedom. Thus, it is important to show respect toward and work with other organizations—even those with whom one has serious religiously based differences. Under pluralism, our religious differences are not a matter of a war against those with whom we disagree. Nor should it be a matter of a war of them against us. Yes, our disagreements are real, and they often invoke strong feelings because they concern serious matters. We do not have to pretend otherwise. But we are not at war with each other and do not disagree about all important things. There is much that is shared across divisions of religious and secular beliefs and convictions. Indeed, one thing we share, or should share, is a commitment to freedom of religion and conscience: asking others to respect our convictions while we in turn respect theirs, and all of us supporting policies that respect the religious or nonreligious convictions of others.

Those coming from a secular perspective should recognize that some of those in need of services might be better helped by an organization with strong religious ties and commitments. And organizations with strong religious ties and commitments should recognize that some secular organizations might be better situated to help some persons with whom they are working. Sometimes referrals are possible and appropriate; other times they may not be. But respect is always possible. We are all in one society, even when we have certain deep differences. This should not be a winner-take-all culture war. Both the secular and the religious need to recognize this and act accordingly.

Possessing and acting on this attitude toward others can help protect the religious freedom of faith-based organizations in two ways. First, it helps demonstrate for all to see that faith-based organizations seeking to protect their religious freedom in the public

---

"The Becket Fund for Religious Liberty is a non-profit, public-interest legal and educational institute with a mission to protect the free expression of all faiths. . . . We like to say we've defended the religious rights of people from 'A to Z,' from Anglicans to Zoroastrians."[6] —From the mission statement of the Becket Fund for Religious Liberty

realm are not simply another special interest group fighting for their own religious freedom while not caring about the religious freedom of others. This increases their credibility with the public, the news media, and public officials.

Second, sometimes faith-based organizations—when they have shown respect toward persons and organizations of other faith traditions and toward completely secular groups—can find support from unlikely sources. Recall the sidebar we included in chapter 7 that quoted from a legal brief the organization Gays and Lesbians for Individual Liberty filed before the Supreme Court. This brief defended the right of a student chapter of the Christian Legal Society to have official on-campus recognition. This perhaps was an unlikely ally, but it was an ally nonetheless. Such allies are made more likely as faith-based organizations of a variety of religious traditions show respect for and are willing to work with each other—and with nonreligious organizations.

Get to Know Community Leaders

It is important for community leaders, in and out of government, to be familiar with an organization and the good that it does in the community. When that is the case, they are less likely to be misled by deceptive labels such as "fundamentalist" or to believe a faith-based organization is engaged in "a war on women" or similar caricatures. When one is not acquainted with a group, it is easy to make inaccurate assumptions about it and what it is doing. Letting influential people know who you are and the good work you are doing in the community is likely to become more important as society as a whole moves away from traditional, religiously based sexual conduct ethics on issues such as abortion, premarital sex, contraceptives, and same-sex marriage.

Invite city council members, the mayor, state legislators, the president of the local community college, the superintendent of the public schools, the editor of the local paper, the head of the Chamber of Commerce, and other such leaders to visit your organization. Explain what you are about, how your faith commitments inform your work, and the contributions you make to the community. And do this before some special issue or controversy has arisen.

I (Stephen) was a state legislator for eight years, and it always struck me how some community groups did a great job of getting in contact, building bridges, and explaining what they were all about. Others did not. Then when some issue or question arose, those community organizations, including faith-based ones, that had previously been in contact with me and other community leaders were in a much better position to present their case and win sympathetic support.

Too often faith-based organizations do not invest the time and effort it takes to get to know community leaders. And then, when a religious freedom issue arises, they quickly run to the media or the lawyers when the whole problem might have been avoided with a little friendly bridge building.

Work with Others to Defend Everyone's Religious Freedom Rights

Finally, it is important for faith-based organizations to work with other faith-based organizations and with umbrella organizations to defend their religious freedom rights. You are not alone, and you should not try to act alone.

Most faith-based organizations have umbrella organizations—both statewide and national—dedicated to helping organizations of a certain type to work together. There are organizations composed of faith-based international aid and relief agencies, faith-based colleges and universities, family service organizations, urban rescue missions, and so on. Catholic Charities is an umbrella organization of many state-level and local Catholic social welfare agencies. All of these have concerns beyond religious freedom issues, but they also include religious freedom issues among their concerns. Being involved in them is a good way to learn about religious freedom issues and, when these issues arise, to be ready to work together. There is truth in the old adage, "There is strength in numbers."

There are also organizations more specifically designed to defend organizational religious freedom rights. Both the Becket Fund for Religious Liberty and the Alliance Defending Freedom specialize in defending faith-based organizations—nonprofit and for-profit alike—whose faith-based practices and commitments have been challenged in court. All faith-based organizations should realize that one day they could find themselves in court, and they should be informed about and be in touch with organizations such as these well before that day.

Being prepared for a courtroom defense, however, is not enough. It is also vital that faith-based organizations anticipate challenges to their religious freedom. They need to be clear in their own minds on the basis for their religious freedom rights. And they need to be prepared to explain to policy makers and the public why religious freedom is vital not only for people and organizations of faith but also for the general public. The public indeed has a stake in the religious freedom of faith-based organizations, since these organizations provide sacrificial services to large segments of the public who are in need.

The Institutional Religious Freedom Alliance or IRFA (www .irfalliance.org), with which we are both involved, works to prepare faith-based organizations to meet challenges to their religious freedom. It is the premier alliance of diverse faith-based organizations working together to protect the religious freedom that all faith-based organizations need in order to flourish *as faith-based organizations*. It does this in three ways. First, it provides training, documentation, and networking resources to help faith-based organizations ensure that they have adopted the best practices

"IRFA promotes government policies, public attitudes, and organizational practices that safeguard institutional religious freedom so that faith-based services can make their vital and uncommon contributions to the common good."[7] —Mission statement of the Institutional Religious Freedom Alliance

to protect their religious freedom. Second, it works in the public policy arena to ensure that laws passed include robust religious freedom protections and exemptions that help prevent cases from going to court in the first place. Third, it works as an alliance to speak on religious freedom issues to help promote a public square that respects organizations of all faiths and protects their religious freedoms.

As more and more faith-based organizations from an ever-wider variety of faith traditions join in this alliance, all of us will be strengthened in our efforts to put principled pluralism into practice and to protect the religious freedom rights of all organizations. As that happens, our nation will experience a renewal of religious freedom for all faiths.

Selected Resources

Key Articles and Chapters

Baptist Joint Committee for Religious Liberty. *The Religious Freedom Restoration Act: 20 Years of Protecting Our First Freedom.* 2013. http://bjconline.org/wp-content/uploads/2014/04/RFRA-Book-FINAL.pdf.

Berg, Thomas. "Progressive Arguments for Religious Organizational Freedom: Reflections on the HHS Mandate." University of St. Thomas Legal Studies Research Paper No. 13–20. 2013. http://papers.ssrn.com/sol3/papers.cfm?abstract_id=2268824.

Campbell, David. "The Challenge of Diversity." *Principled Pluralism: Report of the Inclusive America Project*, June, 2013. http://www.aspeninstitute.org/sites/default/files/content/docs/jsp/Principled-Pluralism.pdf, 43–55.

Colby, Kimberlee. "A Perpetual Haven: Why the Religious Freedom Restoration Act Matters." *Public Discourse*, June 30, 2014. http://www.thepublicdiscourse.com/2014/06/13391/.

Garnett, Richard. "Religious Freedom and the Nondiscrimination Norm." Notre Dame Legal Studies Paper No. 12–65. 2012. http://papers.ssrn.com/sol3/papers.cfm?abstract_id=2087599.

Laycock, Douglas. "Religious Liberty and the Culture Wars." Virginia Public Law and Legal Theory Research Paper No. 2013–23. 2014. http://papers.ssrn.com/sol3/papers.cfm?abstract_id=2304427.

Rienzi, Mark. "God and the Profits: Is There Religious Liberty for Money-Makers?" CUA Columbus School of Law Legal Studies Research Paper No. 2013-17. 2013. http://papers.ssrn.com/sol3/papers.cfm?abstract_id=2229632.

Key Books

Chaplin, Jonathan. *Talking God: The Legitimacy of Religious Public Reasoning*. London: Theos, 2008. Available at http://www.theosthink tank.co.uk/files/files/Reports/TalkingGod1.pdf.

Colombo, Ronald. *The First Amendment and the Business Corporation* (New York: Oxford University Press, 2015).

Esbeck, Carl, Stanley Carlson-Thies, and Ron Sider. *The Freedom of Faith-Based Organizations to Staff on a Religious Basis*. Annapolis, MD: Center for Public Justice, 2004.

Hasson, Kevin Seamus. *The Right to Be Wrong: Ending the Culture War over Religion in America*. San Francisco: Encounter Books, 2005.

Inazu, John. *Confident Pluralism* (forthcoming).

Monsma, Stephen. *Pluralism and Freedom: Faith-Based Organizations in a Democratic Society*. Lanham, MD: Rowman and Littlefield, 2012 (paperback edition, 2014).

Monsma, Stephen. *Putting Faith in Partnerships: Welfare-to-Work in Four Cities*. Ann Arbor, MI: University of Michigan Press, 2004.

Vischer, Robert. *Conscience and the Common Good: Reclaiming the Space Between Person and State*. New York: Cambridge University Press, 2010.

Notes

Chapter 1: A Vision for Our Nation

1. From Justice Stewart's dissenting opinion in *Abington v. Schempp*, 374 U.S. 203 (1963), 319–20.

2. United States Conference of Catholic Bishops Ad Hoc Committee on Religious Liberty, "Our First, Most Cherished Liberty" (Washington, DC: U.S. Conference of Catholic Bishops, 2012), 2.

3. Michael W. McConnell, "Falling Short of Our Ideals," in *Is Religious Freedom Under Threat in America?* (Washington, DC: Religious Freedom Project, Berkley Center for Religion, Peace, and World Affairs, Georgetown University, 2011), 16. Also available at www.nytimes.com/roomfordebate/2011/12/22/is-americans-reli gious-freedom-under-threat/falling-short-of-our-ideals.

4. Michael Wear, "The Changing Face of Christian Politics," *The Atlantic*, February 17, 2014. Available at http://www.theatlantic.com/politics/archive/2014/02 /the-changing-face-of-christian-politics/283859/.

5. Pope Francis, *The Joy of the Gospel (Evangelii Gaudium)* (Washington, DC: U.S. Conference of Catholic Bishops, 2013), 122.

6. Pope Benedict XVI, *Deus Caritas Est (God Is Love)* (2005), 22, 25. Available at http://www.vatican.va/holy_father/benedict_xvi/encyclicals/documents/hf_ben-xvi _enc_20051225_deus-caritas-est_en.html.

7. Richard Stearns, *The Hole in Our Gospel* (Nashville: Thomas Nelson, 2009), 3, 4. Italics in original.

8. Michelle Obama, "Remarks by the First Lady at the African Methodist Episcopal Church Conference," June 28, 2012. Available at http://www.whitehouse.gov /blog/2012/06/30/first-lady-michelle-obama-african-methodist-episcopal-churchs -general-conference.

9. Rick Warren, "If the Contraceptive Mandate Passes, It Will Ruin a Core U.S. Ideology," *Washington Post*, March 21, 2014. Available at http://www.washington post.com/opinions/religious-liberty-is-americas-first-freedom/2014/03/21/498c0048 -b128-11e3-a49e-76adc9210f19_story.html.

10. See Lester M. Salamon, *America's Nonprofit Sector: A Primer*, 2nd ed. (New York: Foundation Center, 1999), and Lester M. Salamon, ed., *The State of Nonprofit America* (Washington, DC: Brookings, 2012).

11. Michael O'Neill, *The Third America: The Emergence of the Nonprofit Sector in the United States* (San Francisco: Jossey-Bass, 1989), 20.

12. Salamon, *America's Nonprofit Sector*, 149. The importance of the role played by religiously based nonprofit organizations in the United States today has also been demonstrated by Stephen V. Monsma, *Pluralism and Freedom: Faith-Based Organizations in a Democratic Society* (Lanham, MD: Rowman & Littlefield, 2012), chap. 2.

Chapter 2: When Religious Organizations Are Said Not to Be Religious

1. *Alpha Delta Chi-Delta Chapter v. Reed*, U.S. Court of Appeals for the Ninth Circuit, 648 F.3d 790 (2011), 9996. Available at http://cdn.ca9.uscourts.gov/datastore /opinions/2011/08/02/09-55299.pdf.

2. Brief for *amici curiae* American Center for Law and Justice and InterVarsity Christian Fellowship/USA in support of Petitioners in *Alpha Delta Chi-Delta Chapter v. Reed* (No. 11-744), 7. Available at http://c0391070.cdn2.cloudfiles.rackspace cloud.com/pdf/aclj-intervarsity-christian-fellowship-alpha-delta-chi-delta-v-reed -amicus-brief-supreme-court.pdf.

3. Judge Kenneth Ripple in a concurring opinion. *Alpha Delta Chi-Delta Chapter v. Reed*, 10005. In this opinion Judge Ripple makes clear he personally would have decided in favor of the student groups but felt bound by precedent.

4. See http://newscenter.sdsu.edu/lead/Default.aspx.

5. *Alpha Delta Chi-Delta Chapter v. Reed*, 10005. See Judge Kenneth Ripple's concurring opinion as quoted in the sidebar.

6. Gary A. Tobin and Aryeh K. Weinberg, *Religious Beliefs and Behavior of College Faculty* (San Francisco: Institute for Jewish and Community Research, 2007), 12.

7. Tish Warren, "The Possibility of Pluralism—Faith and Diversity at Vanderbilt." Available at http://intervarsityatvanderbilt.wordpress.com/2012/04/13/the-possibility -of-pluralism-faith-and-diversity-at-vanderbilt/.

8. *Alpha Delta Chi-Delta Chapter v. Reed*, 9999.

9. Ibid., 9987.

10. Alex Hill, "Pluralism at Risk: The University as a Case Study," in *Principled Pluralism: Report of the Inclusive American Project* (Washington, DC: The Aspen Institute, Justice Society Program, June 2013), 65–66. Available at http://www.aspen institute.org/sites/default/files/content/docs/jsp/Principled-Pluralism.pdf.

11. See http://www.intervarsity.org/page/campus-challenges. For a thoughtful analysis and background information on the challenges InterVarsity organizations are facing on many campuses, see Andy Crouch, "Campus Collisions," http://www .christianitytoday.com/ct/2003/october/6.60.html.

12. Nicholas D. Kristof, "Learning from the Sins of Sodom," *New York Times*, February 28, 2010, wk11. Available at http://www.nytimes.com/2010/02/28/opinion /28kristof.html?_r=0.

13. See www.worldvision.org/content.nsf/about/who-we-are.

14. Interview by Stephen Monsma with Steven McFarland, chief legal counsel of World Vision, May 24, 2010.

15. The case is *Silvia Spencer, Vicki Hulse, and Ted Youngberg v. World Vision,* United States Court of Appeals for the Ninth Circuit, August 23, 2010 (No. 08-35532). Available at http://cdn.ca9.uscourts.gov/datastore/opinions/2010/08/23/08-35532.pdf. For a summary of the court case and its background see Kevin J. Jones, "Federal Court Rejects Case Charging World Vision with Religious Discrimination," EWTN News, January 27, 2011. Available at www.ewtnnews.com/catholic-news/US.php?id=2521.

16. See *Corporation of Presiding Bishop v. Amos,* 483 U.S. 327 (1987).

17. Eric W. from the World Vision website. See http://www.worldvision.org/about -us/job-opportunities/working-for-world-vision.

18. From the dissenting opinion of Judge Marsha S. Berzon in *Silvia Spencer, Vicki Hulse, and Ted Youngberg v. World Vision,* 12597. Italics in original.

19. Berzon in *Silvia Spencer, Vicki Hulse, and Ted Youngberg v. World Vision,* 12599.

20. See its website www.lomalindahealth./org/medical-center/about-us/index/page.

21. Douglas Laycock, "Testimony of Douglas Laycock," in "Faith-Based Initiatives: Recommendations of the President's Advisory Council on Faith-Based and Community Partnerships and Other Current Issues," hearing before the Subcommittee on the Constitution, Civil Rights, and Civil Liberties, Committee on the Judiciary, House of Representatives (November 18, 2010), 35. Available at http://judiciary.house.gov /hearings/printers/111th/111-156_62343.PDF.

22. *Silvia Spencer, Vicki Hulse, and Ted Youngberg v. World Vision,* United States Court of Appeals for the Ninth Circuit, No. 08-35532. Amicus brief for Christian Legal Society et al., 5. Available at http://www.clsnet.org/document.doc?id=205.

23. Quoted in "Congress Should Reject Conservative Religious Groups' Call for Taxpayer-Funded Job Bias, Says American United," Americans United for the Separation of Church and State, August 25, 2010. Available at https://www.au.org/media /press-releases/congress-should-reject-conservative-religious-groups%E2%80%99 -call-for-taxpayer-funded.

Chapter 3: When Laws and Religious Convictions Clash

1. James Madison, "Memorial and Remonstrance against Religious Assessments" (1785). Available at http://religiousfreedom.lib.virginia.edu/sacred/madison_m&r _1785.html.

2. State of Arizona, Senate, 49th Legislature, Second Regular Session, 2010, SB 1070, Sec. 13-2929. Available at http://www.azleg.gov/legtext/49leg/2r/bills/sb1070s.pdf.

3. Brief of the U.S. Conference of Catholic Bishops, the Evangelical Lutheran Church in America, Lutheran Immigration and Refugee Service, and Rev. Gradye Parsons as Stated Clerk of the General Assembly of the Presbyterian Church (USA) as *amici curiae* in support of respondent in *Arizona v. United States* (March 26, 2012), 9. Available at http://www.usccb.org/about/general-counsel/amicus-briefs/upload /state-of-arizona-v-united-states-of-america.pdf.

4. Brief of the U.S. Conference of Catholic Bishops, 31.

5. Brief of the U.S. Conference of Catholic Bishops, 27.

6. From a letter by Rev. Robert J. Baker.

7. See State of Alabama, Legislature, HB 56 (2011). Available at http://latindispatch .com/2011/06/09/text-of-alabama-immigration-law-hb-56/.

8. From a letter by Rev. Robert J. Baker, Catholic Bishop of Birmingham, in which Archbishop Thomas J. Rodi of the Catholic Archdiocese of Mobile, Bishop Henry N.

Parsley of the Episcopal Diocese of Alabama, and Bishop William H. Willimon of the North Alabama Conference of the United Methodist Church joined. Available at http://www.justiceforimmigrants.org/documents/Bishop-Baker-Birmingham-Im migration-Letter.pdf.

9. See *Arizona v. United States*, 567 U.S. _____ (2012) (available at http://www .supremecourt.gov/opinions/11pdf/11-182b5e1.pdf), and *Alabama v. United States*, United States Court of Appeals for the 11th Circuit (August 20, 2012) (available at http://www.ca11.uscourts.gov/opinions/ops/201114532.pdf).

10. Laurie Goodstein, "Bishops Say Rules on Gay Parents Limit Freedom of Religion," *New York Times*, September 28, 2011. Available at www.nytimes.com/2011 /12/29/us/for-bishops-a-battle-over-whose-rights-prevail.htm.

11. Illinois Religious Freedom Protection and Civil Union Act (750 ILCS 75). Available at www.ilga.gov/legislation/ilcs/ilcs3.asp?ActID=3294&ChapterID=59.

12. Second Amended and Supplemental Complaint for Declaratory Judgment, *Catholic Charities v. State of Illinois*, Circuit Court, 7th Judicial Circuit, Sangamon County, Illinois (Case No. 2011 MR 254), 7. Italics in original. Available at https://www .thomasmoresociety.org/wp-content/uploads/2012/01/110726-il-cc-2d-amd-supp-cplt .pdf. Boldface emphasis in original changed to italics.

13. Brief of *amicus curiae* Evangelical Child and Family Agency in support of Plaintiffs' Motion for Summary Judgment, in *Catholic Charities v. State of Illinois*, Circuit Court, 7th Judicial Circuit, Sangamon County, Illinois (Case No. 2011 MR 254), 8. Available at https://www.thomasmoresociety.org/wp-content/uploads/2012/01/110804 -il-cc-ECFA-Supp-P-Mtn-Summ-1.pdf.

14. On the 2,000 number see Doug Finke, "Catholic Charities, DCFS Debate 'Property Right,'" *Peoria Journal Star*, August 18, 2011. Available at http://www .pjstar.com/article/20110818/NEWS/308189873/0/SEARCH.

15. Quoted in Doug Finke, "Catholic Charities Drops Challenge in Adoption Dispute," *Peoria Journal Star*, November 15, 2011. Available at http://www.pjstar .com/article/20111115/NEWS/311159960.

16. Quoted in Manya A. Brachear, "Last Faith Agency Opposed to Civil Union Adoptions Out of Foster Care," *Chicago Tribune*, November 16, 2011. Available at http://articles.chicagotribune.com/2011-11-16/news/ct-met-evangelical-foster-care -gone-20111116_1_ken-withrow-faith-agency-catholic-charities-agencies.

17. From the complaint filed by Notre Dame in *University of Notre Dame v. Kathleen Sebelius*, in the United States District Court for the Northern District of Indiana, Case No. 3:12-CV-253-JTM-CAN (May 21, 2012), para. 137. Available at http:// uc.nd.edu/assets/69013/hhs_complaint.pdf. The internal quotation is from *Ex corde ecclesiae* (*From the Heart of the Church*), which is Pope John Paul II's 1990 apostolic constitution that defines the role and mission of Catholic colleges and universities.

18. "Statement of Faith and Educational Purpose." Available at http://www.wheaton .edu/About-Wheaton/Statement-of-Faith-and-Educational-Purpose.

19. Pope John Paul II, *Ex corde ecclesiae* 1. Internal quotation marks removed. Available at http://www.vatican.va/holy_father/john_paul_ii/apost_constitutions /documents/hf_jp-ii_apc_15081990_ex-corde-ecclesiae_en.html.

20. Whether these "emergency contraceptives" and IUDs work by preventing ovulation or by preventing the implantation of an already fertilized egg in the uterus is in dispute. There is in fact scientific evidence they may work by preventing the

implantation of an already fertilized egg. In fact, the patient pamphlet approved by the Food and Drug Administration (FDA) for ella states: "It is possible that ella may also work by preventing attachment (implantation) to the uterus." See http://www.access data.fda.gov/drugsatfda_docs/label/2010/022474s000lbl.pdf. Also, the American College of Obstetricians and Gynecologists has stated in response to proposed "personhood" proposals that would declare personhood begins when fertilization occurs that "they all attempt to give full legal rights to a fertilized egg by defining 'personhood' from the moment of fertilization. . . . Thus, some of the most effective and reliable forms of contraception, such as oral contraceptives, intrauterine devices (IUDs), and other forms of FDA-approved hormonal contraceptives could be banned in states that adopt 'personhood' measures." Available at http://www.acog.org/About_ACOG/News _Room/News_Releases/2012/Personhood_Measures.

21. Robert P. George and Hamza Yusuf, "Religious Exemptions Are Vital for Religious Liberty," *Wall Street Journal*, March 23, 2014.

22. Notre Dame's complaint in *University of Notre Dame v. Kathleen Sebelius*, para. 1 and 3.

23. Notre Dame's complaint in *University of Notre Dame v. Kathleen Sebelius*, para. 3.

24. Memorandum of Law in Support of Motion for Preliminary Injunction in *Wheaton College v. Sebelius*, U.S. District Court for the District of Columbia, Case No. 1:12-cv-01169, 1. Available at http://sblog.s3.amazonaws.com/wp-content/up loads/2012/08/Wheaton-College-ACA-mandate-plea-8-1-12.pdf.

25. Memorandum of Law, 6.

26. Memorandum of Law, 24–25.

27. See http://www.becketfund.org/scotusvacatesnotredame and http://www.becket fund.org/wp-content/uploads/2014/07/13A1284.pdf.

28. See Becket Fund for Religious Liberty, "HHS Mandate Information Central." Available at http://www.becketfund.org/hhsinformationcentral/.

29. The information on the events reported here come from Jerry Markon, "Health, Abortion Issues Split Obama Administration and Catholic Groups," *Washington Post*, October 31, 2011 (available at http://articles.washingtonpost.com/2011-10-31 /politics/35278788_1_hhs-mandate-catholic-groups-catholic-bishops); "USCCB Files Freedom-of-Information Request over HHS Grant Deal," November 9, 2011 (available at http://www.catholicculture.org/news/headlines/index.cfm?storyid=12304); and the Federal District Court decision by Judge Richard Stearns in *ACLU of Massachusetts v. Sebelius*, No. 09-10038-RGS (March 23, 2012) (available at https://www .aclu.org/files/assets/usccb_decision.pdf).

30. Markon, "Health, Abortion Issues."

31. Markon, "Health, Abortion Issues."

32. It should be noted that on appeal the Federal Court of Appeals for the First District did not uphold the District Court's finding of an unconstitutional establishment of religion, but neither did it reverse that portion of the District Court's decision. Instead, it dismissed the case because the earlier contract of the USCCB with HHS had ended. It thus held the issue was "moot," or no longer proper for a judicial remedy. See *ACLU of Massachusetts v. USCCB, Sebelius, and Sheldon*, U.S. Court of Appeals for the First District, Nos. 12-1466, 12-1658 (January 15, 2013) (available at https://www.aclu.org/files/assets/01.15.13_opinion.pdf).

33. Quoted in "USCCB Files Freedom-of-Information Request over HHS Grant Deal."

34. Markon, "Health, Abortion Issues."

35. "Bishops Appeal Federal Decision That U.S. Constitution Forbids Religious Accommodation, Requires Abortion, Contraception Funding in Anti-Trafficking Service Contract" (April 17, 2012). Available at http://www.usccb.org/news/2012/12-064.cfm.

36. Judge Richard Stearns in *ACLU of Massachusetts v. Sebelius*, 28.

37. Quoting from the District Court decision by Judge Richard Stearns in *ACLU of Massachusetts v. USCCB, Sebelius, and Sheldon*, 21.

38. Executive Order 11478 (July 21, 2014), published in the *Federal Register*, vol. 79, no. 141 (July 23, 2014), pp. 42971–72.

Chapter 4: Can a For-Profit Business Have a Religious Conscience?

1. Sally Steenland, "Faith in Values: Hobby Lobby's Win Is a Loss for Religious Liberty," Center for American Progress, July 16, 2014. Available at http://www.american progress.org/issues/religion/news/2014/07/16/93874/hobby-lobbys-win-is-a-loss-for-religious-liberty/.

2. The information on the case was gathered from the following sources: Alan Rappeport, "Hobby Lobby Made Fight a Matter of Christian Principles," *New York Times*, June 30, 2014 (available at http://www.nytimes.com/2014/07/01/us/hobby-lobby-made-fight-a-matter-of-christian-principle.html); *Burwell v. Hobby Lobby Stores*, 573 U.S. _____ (2014) (available at http://www.supremecourt.gov/opinions/13pdf/13-354_olp1 .pdf); Brief for the Respondents, Supreme Court of the United States, No, 13-354, *Sebelius v. Hobby Lobby Stores* (available at http://sblog.s3.amazonaws.com/wp-content /uploads/2013/10/No-13-354-Brief-for-Respondents.pdf); Brief for the Petitioners, Supreme Court of the United States, No, 13-354, *Sebelius v. Hobby Lobby Stores* (available at http://sblog.s3.amazonaws.com/wp-content/uploads/2014/01/01.12.14_brief_for _petitioners_doj.pdf); Becket Fund for Religious Liberty, "Sebelius versus Hobby Lobby" (available at www.becketfund.org/hobbylobby).

3. Ethan Bronner, "A Flood of Suits Fights Coverage of Birth Control," *New York Times*, January 27, 2013, 1 and 11. Available at http://www.nytimes.com/2013/01/27 /health/religious-groups-and-employers-battle-contraception-mandate.html.

4. Quoted in Rappeport, "Hobby Lobby Made Fight a Matter of Christian Principles."

5. The mission statement is available at http://retailindustry.about.com/od/retail bestpractices/ig/Company-Mission-Statements/Hobby-Lobby-Stores-Mission-State ment.htm.

6. Quoted in Rappeport, "Hobby Lobby Made Fight a Matter of Christian Principles."

7. As we saw earlier in chap. 3, there is certain scientific evidence in support of the Greens' position. See chapter 3n20. In addition, the Supreme Court has also held that the four birth control measures to which Hobby Lobby objected "may have the effect of preventing an already fertilized egg from developing any further by inhibiting its attachment to the uterus." *Burwell v. Hobby Lobby*, majority opinion, 8.

8. Quoted in the District Court opinion. *Hobby Lobby Stores v. Sebelius*, U.S. District Court, W.D. Oklahoma (No. CIV-12-1000-HE), 2. Available at http://scholar .google.com/scholar_case?case=10390225281706554853.

9. Quoted in *Hobby Lobby Stores v. Sebelius*, U.S. District Court, 2.

10. *Hobby Lobby Stores v. Sebelius*, Brief for the Petitioners, 12.

11. For a copy of the Court of Appeals decision see *Hobby Lobby Stores v. Sebelius*, U.S. Court of Appeals, Tenth Circuit (No. 12-6294). Available at http://www.ca10 .uscourts.gov/opinions/12/12-6294.pdf.

12. *Burwell v. Hobby Lobby Stores*, majority opinion by Justice Alito, 18. Italics in original.

13. *Burwell v. Hobby Lobby Stores*, dissenting opinion by Justice Ginsburg, 32.

14. *New York Times*, July 1, 2014, A16.

15. Carmel Martin and Joshua Field, "Re-Establishing Religious Liberty Post–*Hobby Lobby*," Center for American Progress (June 30, 2014). Available at http://www .americanprogress.org/issues/civil-liberties/news/2014/06/30/92665/re-establishing -religious-liberty-post-hobby-lobby/.

16. Justice Anthony Kennedy, *Burwell v. Hobby Lobby Stores*, concurring opinion, 2. Internal reference removed.

17. Martin and Field, "Re-Establishing Religious Liberty Post–*Hobby Lobby*." Italics added.

18. David Brooks, "The Orthodox Surge," *New York Times*, March 7, 2013. Available at http://www.nytimes.com/2013/03/08/opinion/brooks-the-orthodox-surge.html.

19. Mark Renzi, "God and the Profits: Is There Religious Liberty for Money-Makers?" (2013), 2. Available at http://papers.ssrn.com/sol3/papers.cfm?abstract _id=2229632.

20. See http://benjerry.com/about-us/b-corp.

21. For a helpful paper that develops this position much more fully than we do here, see Renzi, "God and the Profits: Is There Religious Liberty for Money-Makers?"

22. Mary Ann Glendon, "Free Businesses to Act with Conscience," *Boston Globe*, December 8, 2013. Available at http://www.bostonglobe.com/opinion/2013/12/08 /should-business-have-conscience/cK6o6G6dwrWeRJjk1uPVYM/story.html.

23. *Burwell v. Hobby Lobby Stores*, majority opinion by Justice Alito, 23.

24. A compelling and clear argument for why some businesses should be extended religious freedom and other First Amendment rights is offered in a recent book, Ronald J. Colombo, *The First Amendment and the Business Corporation* (New York: Oxford University Press, 2015).

25. See http://www.crossway.org/about/ and http://www.tyndale.com/50_Company /tyndale_purpose.php.

26. Brief for the Respondents, 31–32. Internal references removed.

27. See, for example, the account of an Albuquerque wedding photographer whom the New Mexico Supreme Court held in violation of New Mexico's nondiscrimina-tion laws for refusing on religious grounds to photograph a same-sex commitment ceremony. Available at http://www.outsidethebeltway.com/court-holds-that-wedding -photographer-cannot-refuse-service-to-gay-couples/. In 2014 the United States Su-preme Court decided not to hear this case, leaving the New Mexico decision to stand.

28. Michael Paulson, "Can't Have Your Cake, Gays Are Told, and a Rights Battle Rises," *New York Times* (December 16, 2014), A1, A17. Available at http://www .nytimes.com/2014/12/16/us/cant-have-your-cake-gays-are-told-and-a-rights-battle -rises.html?_r=0.

29. Julia Mirabella and Sandhya Bathija "*Hobby Lobby v. Sebelius*: Crafting a Dangerous Precedent," Center for American Progress (October 1, 2013), 6. Available

at http://www.americanprogress.org/issues/civil-liberties/report/2013/10/01/76033
/hobby-lobby-v-sebelius-crafting-a-dangerous-precedent/.
　30. *Burwell v. Hobby Lobby Stores*, dissenting opinion by Justice Ginsburg, 29.
　31. *Burwell v. Hobby Lobby Stores*, dissenting opinion by Justice Ginsburg, 29,
33–34.
　32. Mirabella and Bathija, *"Hobby Lobby v. Sebelius*: Crafting a Dangerous
Precedent," 6.
　33. The major study of how courts have interpreted RFRA mainly concerns state
versions of the protection since almost all of the small number of RFRA court cases
have involved state RFRAs, not the federal law. This study shows that usually the
government is able to demonstrate that it has a compelling interest for the policy it is
pursuing, but then the government must further demonstrate the resulting religious
freedom burden that policy imposes on the company or other religious claimant is
unavoidable. See Christopher Lund, "Religious Liberty after Gonzales: A Look at
State RFRAs," Wayne State University Law School Legal Studies Research Paper
Series, no. 10-12 (August 26, 2010). Available at http://papers.,ssrn.com/sol3/papers
.cfm?absract_id=1666268.

Chapter 5: Common Threads

　1. Rick Warren, "If the Contraceptive Mandate Passes, It Will Ruin a Core U.S.
Ideology," *Washington Post*, March 21, 2014. Available at http://www.washington
post.com/opinions/religious-liberty-is-americas-first-freedom/2014/03/21/498c0048
-b128-11e3-a49e-76adc9210f19_story.html.
　2. Tim Shah and Tom Farr, "Religion in the Public Square," *New York Times*,
December 22, 2011. Available at http://www.nytimes.com/roomfordebate/2011/12
/22/is-americans-religious-freedom-under-threat/defending-religion-in-the-public
-square.
　3. From the dissenting opinion of Judge Marsha S. Berzon in *Sylvia Spencer, Vicki
Hulse, and Ted Youngberg v. World Vision*, United States Court of Appeals for the
Ninth Circuit, No. 08-35532 (filed August 23, 2010), 12599. Available at http://cdn
.ca9.uscourts.gov/datastore/opinions/2010/08/23/08-35532.pdf.
　4. Dorothy Samuels, "Back to First Principles on Religious Freedom," *New York
Times*, February 25, 2012. Available at http://www.nytimes.com/2012/02/26/opinion
/sunday/back-to-first-principles-on-religious-freedom.html.
　5. See the statements by Pope Benedict XVI and Pope Francis quoted earlier in
chap. 1 (5–7).
　6. Jay Michaelson, "Redefining Religious Liberty: The Covert Campaign against
Civil Rights," Political Research Associates (March 2013), 24. Available at http://
www.politicalresearch.org/wp-content/uploads/downloads/2013/04/PRA_Redefining
-Religious-Liberty_March2013_PUBLISH.pdf.
　7. Pope Francis, *Evangelii Gaudium* (*The Joy of the Gospel*) (Washington, DC:
U.S. Conference of Catholic Bishops, 2013), 19–20.
　8. SEC. 2000e-1(a) of the 1964 Civil Rights Act, as amended in 1972 (Section 702).
Available at http://www.eeoc.gov/laws/statutes/titlevii.cfm.
　9. See *Corporation of Presiding Bishop v. Amos*, 483 U.S. 327 (1987).
　10. *Corporation of Presiding Bishop v. Amos*, at 339.

11. ACLU Reproductive Freedom Project, "Religious Refusals and Reproductive Rights" (2002), 11. Available at http://www.aclu.org/FilesPDFs/ACF911.pdf.

12. Michaelson, "Redefining Religious Liberty," 14.

13. Martin Luther King Jr., "I Have a Dream." Available at http://www.archives.gov/press/exhibits/dream-speech.pdf.

14. "In Indiana, Religion as a Cover for Bigotry," *New York Times*, March 31, 2015. Available at www.nytimes.com/2015/03/31/opinion/in-indiana-using-religion-as-a-cover-for-bigotry.html.

15. Richard Garnett, "A Very Bad Religious-Freedom Opinion in Massachusetts," *National Review Online*, March 27, 2012. Available at https://www.nationalreview.com/node/294527.

16. "Motion to Dismiss, or in the Alternative, for Summary Judgment by Intervenors," in *Catholic Charities v. State of Illinois*, Circuit Court for the Seventh Judicial Circuit, Sangamon County, Illinois (Case No. 11-MR-254), 3. Available at http://www.aclu-il.org/wp-content/uploads/2011/07/Motion-to-dismiss-for-SJ-FINAL.pdf.

17. *ACLU of Massachusetts v. USCCB, Sebelius, and Sheldon*, U.S. Court of Appeals for the 1st District, Nos. 12-1466, 12-1658 (January 15, 2013), 25. Available at https://www.aclu.org/files/assets/01.15.13_opinion.pdf.

18. *ACLU of Massachusetts v. USCCB, Sebelius, and Sheldon*, 25.

19. Many books dealing with differing aspects of nonprofit organizations use the term "Independent Sector" in their titles. See, for example, Virginia Ann Hodgkinson, *Dimensions of the Independent Sector: A Statistical Profile* (Washington, DC: Independent Sector, 1989), and Virginia Ann Hodgkinson, *Nonprofit Almanac, 1992–1993: Dimensions of the Independent Sector* (San Francisco: Jossey-Bass, 1992).

20. "IS Vision, Mission, and Values." Available at https://www.independentsector.org/mission_and_values.

21. See http://www.whitehouse.gov/administration/eop/ofbnp.

22. Large parts of the following section are taken from Stephen V. Monsma, afterword to *Pluralism and Freedom: Faith-Based Organizations in a Democratic Society* (Lanham, MD: Rowman & Littlefield, 2014). We thank Rowman & Littlefield for permission to use this material.

23. Molly Worthen, "One Nation under God?," *New York Times*, December 22, 2012. Available at http://www.nytimes.com/2012/12/23/opinion/sunday/american-christianity-and-secularism-at-a-crossroads.html.

24. Michaelson, "Redefining Religious Liberty," 13, 15.

25. See http://www.student-affairs.buffalo.edu/idc/aboutus.php.

26. See http://newscenter.sdsu.edu/lead/Default.aspx.

27. See www.vanderbilt.edu/deanofstudents/mission-purposes.

28. *Lynch v. Donnelly*, 465 U.S. 668 (1984), 716. Underlining present in the original has been removed.

29. Frank Bruni, "Reading God's Mind," *New York Times*, March 4, 2013. Available at http://www.nytimes.com/2013/03/05/opinion/bruni-reading-gods-mind.html.

30. "What American Workers Really Think about Religion: Tanenbaum's 2013 Survey of American Workers and Religion" (New York: Tanenbaum Center for Interreligious Understanding, 2013), 22.

Chapter 6: Free to Serve: Living with Our Differences

1. Jennifer S. Bryson, "Stanford, Marriage and Abortion Controversies, and the Mission of a University," Public Discourse (Witherspoon Institute, March 19, 2014). Available at http://www.thepublicdiscourse.com/2014/03/12913/.

2. A. James Reichley, *Religion in American Political Life* (Washington, DC: Brookings Institution, 1985), 165. Italics in original.

3. For further confirmation that secularism is indeed a perspective on life and the world, see the website of the Freedom from Religion Foundation: http://ffrf.org/. For a more fully developed idea that secularism is not evenhanded or neutral between religion and nonreligion but a point of view that is in competition with various religious points of view, see Stephen V. Monsma, *When Sacred and Secular Mix: Religious Nonprofit Organizations and Public Money* (Lanham, MD: Rowman & Littlefield, 1996), 54–56.

4. James Madison, "Memorial and Remonstrance against Religious Assessments" (1785). Available at many websites, such as http://religiousfreedom.lib.virginia.edu /sacred/madison_m&r_1785.html. The internal quotation is from the Virginia Declaration of Rights of 1776, Article 16.

5. Lester M. Salamon, *America's Nonprofit Sector: A Primer*, 2nd ed. (New York: Foundation Center, 1999), 22.

6. Ross Douthat, "A Company Liberals Could Love," *New York Times*, July 6, 2014, SR11. Available at http://www.nytimes.com/2014/07/06/opinion/sunday/ross -douthat-a-company-liberals-could-love-.html.

7. Nick Spencer, *How to Think about Religious Freedom* (London: Theos, 2014), 17. Available at http://www.theosthinktank.co.uk/files/files/Reports/Religious%20 freedom%20text%206%20combined.pdf.

8. Michael Wear, "The Changing Face of Christian Politics," *The Atlantic*, February 17, 2014. Available at http://www.theatlantic.com/politics/archive/2014/02 /the-changing-face-of-christian-politics/283859/.

9. The massive U.S. Religious Landscape survey by the Pew Forum on Religion and Public Life found 50.2 percent of the American population belonged either to evangelical Protestant churches or the Roman Catholic Church. See http://religions .pewforum.org/affiliations.

Chapter 7: Free to Serve: Faith-Based Organizations in the Public Realm

1. Brief of Gays and Lesbians for Individual Liberty as *amicus curiae* in support of Petitioner in *Christian Legal Society Chapter of The University of California, Hastings College of Law v. Martinez.* Available at http://www.americanbar.org/content /dam/aba/publishing/preview/publiced_preview_briefs_pdfs_09_10_08_1371_Peti tionerAmCuGLIL.authcheckdam.pdf. This Supreme Court case dealt with the ability of the student chapter of the Christian Legal Society at the Hastings law school of the University of California to have religious belief and practice standards for their leaders. Unfortunately, the Supreme Court upheld the school's policy of requiring all on-campus student organizations to admit any and all students as members and leaders.

2. Tish Harrison Warren, "The Possibility of Pluralism—Faith and Diversity at Vanderbilt." Available at http://intervarsityatvanderbilt.wordpress.com.

3. Kelly Cunningham, "Statement Regarding the Status of Asian InterVarsity Christian Fellowship at U-M," (April 12, 2013). Available at http://vpcomm.umich .edu/pa/key/ChristianFellowship.html.

4. Quoted at InterVarsity Christian Fellowship, "Campus Challenges." Available at http://www.intervarsity.org/page/campus-challenges.

5. See http://ffrf.org.

6. See, for example, a *New York Times* editorial, "Faith-Based Discrimination," October 14, 2009 (available at http://www.nytimes.com/2009/10/14/opinion/14wed4 .html) and the website of the advocacy organization, Americans United for the Separation of Church and State (https://www.au.org).

7. The case was *Wisconsin v. Yoder*, 406 U.S. 205 (1972).

8. Church Amendments, 42 U.S.C. §300a-7. Available at http://www.hhs.gov/ocr /civilrights/understanding/ConscienceProtect/42usc300a7.pdf.

9. Eugene Volokh, "A Brief Political History of Religious Exemptions," in a January 21, 2015 *Washington Post* blog posting. Available at http://www.washingtonpost.com /news/volokh-conspiracy/wp/2015/01/21/a-brief-political-history-of-religious-exemp tions/. For more detail on the history of religious exemptions see Douglas Laycock, "Regulatory Exemptions of Religious Behavior and the Original Understanding of the Establishment Clause, *Notre Dame Law Review*, Vol. 81 (2006), 1793-1842. Available at http://scholarship.law.nd.edu/cgi/viewcontent.cgi?article=1358&context=ndlr.

10. Religious Freedom Restoration Act of 1993, Pub. L. No. 103-141. Available at http://www.justice.gov/jmd/ls/legislative_histories/pl103-141/act-pl103-141.pdf.

11. Brief of *amicus curiae*, Evangelical Child and Family Agency in support of Plaintiffs' Motion for Summary Judgment in *Catholic Charities of the Diocese of Springfield-in-Illinois v. State of Illinois*. Available at https://www.thomasmore society.org/wp-content/uploads/2012/01/110804-il-cc-ECFA-Supp-P-Mtn-Summ-1 .pdf.

12. Memorandum of Law in Support of Motion for Preliminary Injunction, in *Wheaton College v. Sebelius*, in the United States District Court for the District of Columbia, 24. Available at http://www.becketfund.org/wp-content/uploads/2012/08 /Wheaton-PI-Memorandum-FINAL.pdf.

13. Complaint and Demand for Jury Trial, *University of Notre Dame v. Sebelius* in the United States District Court for the Northern District of Columbia, 2. Available at http://uc.nd.edu/assets/69013/hhs_complaint.pdf.

14. Rahm Emanuel, "Both Parties Need to Grow Up in Discussing Early Education," *Washington Post*, March 31, 2014. Italics added. Available at http://www .washingtonpost.com/opinions/rahm-emanuel-on-early-education-both-parties-need -to-grow-up/2014/03/31/c7d9e1f0-b6a4-11e3-8cc3-d4bf596577eb_story.html.

15. For the exact provision of the bill and its legislative history see https://www .govtrack.us/congress/bills/113/s815/text.

16. See, e.g., Sarah McBride, et al., *We the People: Why Congress and U.S. States Must Pass Comprehensive LGBT Nondiscrimination Provisions* (Washington, DC: Center for American Progress, December 2014).

17. Niraj Chokshi, "Gay rights, religious rights and a compromise in an unlikely place: Utah," *Washington Post*, April 12, 2015. Available at http://www.washington post.com/politics/gay-rights-religious-rights-and-a-compromise-in-an-unlikely-place -utah/2015/04/12/39278b12-ded8-11e4-a500-1c5bb-1c5bb1d8ff6a_story.html.

Chapter 8: Five Questions

1. Kevin Seamus Hasson, *The Right to Be Wrong: Ending the Culture War over Religion in America* (San Francisco: Encounter Books, 2005), 15.
2. Ibid.
3. Tish Harrison Warren, "The Possibility of Pluralism—Faith and Diversity at Vanderbilt." Available at http://intervarsityatvanderbilt.wordpress.com.
4. "Faith-Based Discrimination," *New York Times*, October 14, 2009.
5. See Tobin Grant, "Why No One Understands Indiana's New Religous Freedom Law," *Washington Post*, March 30, 2015.
6. Chief Justice John Roberts, *Hosanna-Tabor v. EEOC*, 565 U.S. _____ (2012). Opinion of the Court, 21. Available at http://www.supremecourt.gov/opinions/11 pdf/10-553.pdf.
7. Religious Freedom Restoration Act of 1993, Pub. L. No. 103-141. By way of legal precedents the "compelling state interest" test is a high bar that is not easy for governmental actions to clear.
8. Marc Stern, Thomas Berg, and Douglas Laycock, amicus brief for the American Jewish Committee in *Hollingsworth v. Perry* and the *United States v. Windsor*. Available at https://www.glad.org/uploads/docs/cases/windsor-v-united-states/amicus -brief-of-american-jewish-committee.pdf, 15.
9. This statement was by Justice Elena Kagan made by her during oral argument in the *Burwell v. Hobby Lobby Stores* case. See http://www.supremecourt.gov /oral_arguments/argument_transcripts/13-354_5436.pdf.
10. See http://www.saudiembassy.net/about/country-information/Islam/five_pillars _of_Islam.aspx.
11. Douglas Laycock, ed., *Religious Liberty* (Grand Rapids: Eerdmans, 2010), 1:13.
12. *Rosenberger v. Rector*, 515 U.S. 819, at 839 (1995). More developed explanations and defenses of this understanding of religious freedom under the First Amendment can be found in Stephen V. Monsma, *Pluralism and Freedom: Faith-Based Organizations in a Democratic Society* (Lanham, MD: Rowman & Littlefield, 2012), especially 61–64.

Chapter 10: How Faith-Based Organizations Can Protect Their Religious Freedom

1. *Silvia Spencer, Vicki Hulse, and Ted Youngberg v. World Vision*, United States Court of Appeals for the Ninth Circuit, August 23, 2010 (No. 08-35532), 12550. Available at http://cdn.ca9.uscourts.gov/datastore/opinions/2010/08/23/08-35532.pdf.
2. *Burwell v. Hobby Lobby Stores*, 573 U.S. _____ (2014). Opinion of the Court, 4. Available at http://www.supremecourt.gov/opinions/13pdf/13-354_olp1.pdf.
3. From the complaint filed by Notre Dame in *University of Notre Dame v. Kathleen Sebelius*, in the United States District Court for the Northern District of Indiana, Case No. 3:12-CV-253-JTM-CAN (May, 21 2012), para. 3. Available at http://uc.nd.edu /assets/69013/hhs_complaint.pdf.
4. The following report is based on Sherry F. Colb, "The New Mexico Supreme Court Applies Anti-Discrimination Law to Wedding Photographer Refusing to Photograph Same-Sex Commitment Ceremonies," available at http://verdict.justia.com/2013/09/04 /new-mexico-supreme-court-anti-discrimination-law-to-wedding-photographer and

the New Mexico Supreme Court's decision in this case, available at http://www.nm compcomm.us/nmcases/nmsc/slips/SC33,687.pdf.

    5. Justice Richard C. Bosson, concurring opinion in *Elane Photography v. Willock*, para. 87. Justice Bosson joined with the court's majority in what we view as the wrong decisions in this case. He did, however, show a commendable empathy toward the Huguenins and the dilemma New Mexico law, as interpreted and applied by the court, put them in. Available at http://www.nmcompcomm.us/nmcases/nmsc/slips/SC33,687.pdf.

    6. http://www.becketfund.org/our-mission/.

    7. http://www.irfalliance.org/.

Index